Evolution, Purpose, and Values in Economics

Principles of Economics for the Information Age

Jenden Hunt

Evolution, Purpose, and Values in Economics: Principles of Economics for the Information Age.

Table of Contents

Acknowledgments

I AM GRATEFUL for the extensive help my son Joshua Hunt gave me regarding the use of computer software and websites.

A big thank you to Jim Manheim who edited the book. Also, Amnet provided very useful copy editing and formatting services.

Anne Dwyer, a Muscle Activation Technique (MAT) therapist, continually encouraged me to keep working on the manuscript, and my friend Kathy Bloch's suggestion contributed to a revision of the book. Ben Levi provided helpful comments regarding the application of the Spiral Dynamics theory.

Philosopher Ken Wilber's books inspired me to apply integral theory to economics.

Rudolf Steiner's ideas on the Threefold State are a major contribution to this book.

And I am extremely grateful for the permission granted by Gail Hochachka to extensively quote her in Chapter 6. Essentially, I am mainly presenting her ideas in condensed form in that chapter of the book.

Karen Bailey is responsible for the beautiful cover design for the book.

Christine Tracy edited the back cover and Marl Anzicek made comments that led to the revision of the Minimizing Costs section in Chapter 4 to make it more understandable.

Preface

MOST OF THE material in this book was previously published in 2020 under the title *Evolving Beyond Capitalism and Socialism.* A major proposal of that book regarding moving to nonprofit economic entities has been changed to having these organizations go to a maximum profit of 10%. One of the major reasons to have producers of goods and services go to the nonprofit model was to provide more stability to the economy since markets, and especially the stock market would be less prone to speculation causing ups and downs in the economy. But if one firm in an industry that is dominated by just a few firms went to the nonprofit model, the competitors would most likely be forced to liquidate by the shareholders and this would destabilize an industry and possibly the whole economy. The title of the book has been changed to *Evolution, Purpose, and Values in Economics,* and modifications to the text have been made throughout the book to reflect the change to the 10% maximum profit model. However, an economic organization providing a new product that no one else offers might still want to go the nonprofit route since there would be no competitors that would be forced out of business. Furthermore, some information has been added to make the Minimizing Costs section in the Microeconomics chapter more understandable.

1
Introduction

ROBERT HEILBRONER, WRITING in *The Worldly Philosophers,* thought the book's title described the prominent economists in history.[1] In this spirit, many of the assumptions economists make today will be reexamined, and alternative ways to approach the subject will be explored. Capitalism served its purpose reasonably well in the industrial era. However, we are now in the information age, and it will be proposed here that the integral theories of the philosopher Ken Wilber, the Spiral Dynamics values system of Don Beck and Chris Cowan, the idea of abundance as presented by Louise Hay, Maslow's Hierarchy of Needs, Piaget's Levels of Cognition, and Rudolf Steiner's Threefold Social Order can all be incorporated into expanded principles of economics.

A key proposal for an economic system for the information age is that we move to an alternative business model called purposive enterprise. Product- and service-producing organizations would move from the goal of maximizing profits to one where making the best product or service at an affordable price is emphasized. This would involve voluntarily producing at an output where profits are limited to a maximum of 10%. Purposive enterprises would cover or avoid external costs associated with maintaining the environment, pay a living wage, emphasize the purpose of the organization, and their employees would be working in occupations that fulfill their purpose in life. As economic entities begin acting more responsibly, the government actually would be smaller since there would be less need for regulation.

An additional proposal that would make the government smaller would be for a structure in line with Rudolf Steiner's idea of a Threefold State. Three sectors in society would negotiate with each other. There would be a rights, an economic, and an individual/cultural sector. What now constitutes the government would shrink, for its foremost concern would, under this scenario, be guaranteeing rights to its citizens, thus emerging as the rights sector. In addition to the economic sector, there would be a third part of the social system called individual/cultural, and it would comprise courts, schools, healthcare, and spiritual organizations. The system would gradually evolve, as capitalism did, with minimal law changes to allow it to develop as society grows in consciousness. As the world changes at an ever-faster rate, this may all come to fruition more quickly than one might imagine.

The next chapter will begin by examining the assumptions, especially those regarding values in current economic theory, and give details about purposive enterprise and the Threefold State. It will then go into how this might impact economic theory regarding resources, supply and demand, microeconomics, macroeconomics, and environmental economics, in Chapters 2 to 6. And then conclude in Chapter 7 with a summary of the basic ideas presented.

2

Interior Assumptions and New Solutions

A. Examining Interior Assumptions of Economic Theory

WHAT ARE WE doing when we look at economists' current assumptions? We are taking a look at the interior beliefs behind economic theory. The four quadrants of Ken Wilber's integral philosophical model constitute one way to look at reality. They involve interior I (singular) and We (plural), and exterior It (singular) and Its (plural) spaces. He begins by talking about three dimensions, and then expands the idea to four dimensions:

> And the point is that every event in the manifest world has all three of those dimensions. You can look at any event from the point of view of the "I" (or how I personally see and feel about the event); from the point of view of the "we" (how not just I but others see the event); and as an "it" (or the objective facts of the event).

> Thus, an integrally informed path will therefore take all of those dimensions into account, and thus arrive at a more comprehensive and effective approach—in the "I" and the "we" and the "it"—or in self and culture and nature.

So fundamental are these dimensions of "I," "we," and "it" that we call them the four quadrants, and we make them the foundation of the integral framework . . . (We arrive at "four" quadrants by subdividing "it" into singular "it" and plural "its," as we will see.)[2]

See Figure 1.

	Interior	Exterior
Singular	I	IT
Plural	WE	ITS

Figure 1:[3] The Four Quadrants.

Economics is primarily concerned with the lower-right quadrant, the collective of objective reality, or "Its." For example, it deals with measuring and trying to predict and explain aggregate statistics, such as unemployment and inflation rates for a whole country or other geographic areas. But many of its assumptions are grounded in the left-hand quadrants. For example, economics assumes people act out of rational self-interest. This idea refers to the interior thinking of individuals in the upper-left "I" quadrant. And here is a common definition of economics: "The study of how people allocate their limited resources to satisfy their unlimited wants."[4] The "unlimited wants" may be considered on an individual or collective basis, each of which would apply to the "I" or "We" left-hand quadrants. And "unlimited wants" and "rational self-interest" are current interior economic assumptions that will be examined in detail here.

According to Wilber, another way to look at the quadrants is this: "Instead of saying 'we,' 'it,' and 'I,' what if we said the Good, the True, and the Beautiful?"[5]

And he says, "If you leave out science, or you leave out art, or you leave out morals, something is going to be missing, something will get broken."[6] Science relates to the "True," art to the "Beautiful," and morals to the "Good." See Figure 2.

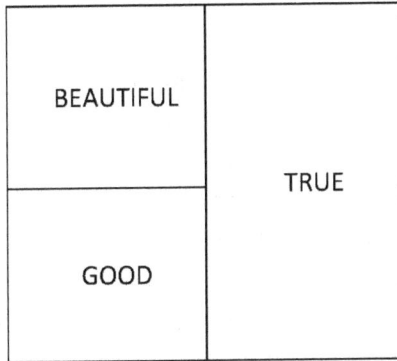

```
┌─────────────┬──────────────────┐
│             │                  │
│  BEAUTIFUL  │                  │
│             │     TRUE         │
├─────────────┤                  │
│             │                  │
│    GOOD     │                  │
│             │                  │
└─────────────┴──────────────────┘
```

Figure 2:[7] The Good, the True, and the Beautiful.

So, while economics is a science that should emphasize the lower-right quadrant, as it currently does, it needs to pay attention to the other quadrants as well. So, for example, although economics currently admits that values cannot completely be taken out of its realm, it rarely examines their influence. But values of the wider culture and of individuals are associated with the left-hand quadrants, and these will be examined.

Reviewing these assumptions, which often relate to the left-hand quadrants, will lead us to look at economics in a different way. Proposals for a new economic system and social structure will then be made. And then, we may hope that economics' search for the truth in the right-hand quadrants will include the beauty and the good, and lead to the further evolution of these three dimensions of reality.

1. Positive and Normative Economics

Economists make a distinction between normative and positive economics. Normative economics involves value statements, such as "everyone should have health insurance." Positive economics relates to if-then statements or statements of fact. If–then statements are ones that can theoretically be tested, such as: if auto production goes down, Michigan unemployment claims will go up. An example of an economic statement of fact would be: "The seasonally adjusted U.S. unemployment rate for June 2014 is 6.1%." Economists try to stay in the positive area of their subject but admit that it is hard to keep values out when talking about the field. Roger Miller, the author of the textbook *Economics Today,* admits that even the choice of what is included in a book involves values.[8] Since values cannot be avoided in discussing economics, and Don Beck and Chris Cowan developed Spiral Dynamics, a theory that details the development of values in cultures and individuals, it will be useful to start applying their work to economics. In addition, the philosopher Ken Wilber's Major Epochs (Social) and cognition levels will be presented, so as to include the major technology, and ways of thinking, that correspond with the different values people hold.

2. Spiral Dynamics and Self-Interest

Economists currently assume that people act in their own rational self-interest. The idea of Spiral Dynamics shows how individuals' and cultures' values change as they develop. Spiral Dynamics can demonstrate that what constitutes self-interest is influenced by a person's values, so the second half of this economic assumption is more complicated than one might think.

Table 1 is a short summary of the valueMEMES of Spiral Dynamics (columns 1–5),[9] correlated with Ken Wilber's Major Epochs (Social) (column 6),[10] Piaget's Cognition Levels (column 7),[11] and Maslow's Hierarchy of Needs (column 8).[12] The Major Epochs (Social) are included because they are associated with a dominant mode of economic production and level of government.

Tier	valueMEME Color/Name	Basic Theme	Yrs. Ago Started	Values	Major Epochs (Social)	Cognition	Needs
First-Tier "Subsistence" valueMEMES	BEIGE/ Instinctive/ Survivalistic	Do what you must just to stay alive	100,000	1. Uses instincts and habits just to survive 2. Distinct self is barely awakened or sustained 3. Food, water, warmth, sex, and safety have priority 4. Forms into survival bands to perpetuate life 5. Lives "off the land" much as other animals		Sensorimotor	Physiological
	PURPLE/ Magical/ Animistic	Keep the spirits happy and the tribe's nest warm and safe	50,000	1. Obeys the desires of the spirit being and mystical signs 2. Shows allegiance to the chief, elders, ancestors, and the clan 3. Individual subsumed in group 4. Preserves sacred objects, places, events, and memories 5. Observes rites of passage, seasonal cycles, and tribal customs	Foraging tribes	Preconceptual preoperational	Beginning of safety
	RED/ Impulsive/ Egocentric	Be what you are and do what you want, regardless	10,000	1. The world is a jungle full of threats and predators 2. Breaks free of any domination or constraint to please self as self desires 3. Stands tall, expects attention, demands respect, and calls the shots 4. Enjoys self to the fullest right now without guilt or remorse 5. Conquers, out-foxes, and dominates other aggressive characters	Organized hunt		Safety
	BLUE/ Purposeful/ Authoritarian	Life has meaning, direction, and purpose with predetermined outcomes	5,000	1. One sacrifices self to the transcendent Cause, Truth, or righteous Pathway 2. The Order enforces a code of conduct based on eternal, absolute principles 3. Righteous living produces stability now and guarantees future reward 4. Impulsivity is controlled through guilt; everybody has their proper place 5. Laws, regulations, and discipline build character and moral fiber	Horticultural village Agrarian early state Advanced agrarian	Concrete operational	Belongingness
	ORANGE/ Achievist/ Strategic	Act in your own self-interest by playing the game to win	300	1. Change and advancement are inherent within the scheme of things 2. Progresses by learning nature's secrets and seeking out best solutions 3. Manipulates Earth's resources to create and spread the abundant good life 4. Optimistic, risk-taking, and self-reliant people deserve success 5. Societies prosper through, strategy, technology, and competitiveness	empire Industrial nation/state	Formal operational	Self-esteem
	GREEN/ Communitarian/ Egalitarian	Seek peace within the inner self and explore, with others, the caring dimensions of community	150	1. The human spirit must be freed from greed, dogma, and divisiveness 2. Feelings, sensitivity, and caring supersede cold rationality 3. Spreads the Earth's resources and opportunities equally among all 4. Reaches decisions through reconciliation and consensus processes 5. Refreshes spirituality, brings harmony, and enriches human development			Self-actualization
Second-Tier "Being" valueMEMES	YELLOW/ Integrative	Live fully and responsibly as what you are and learn to become	50	1. Life is a kaleidoscope of natural hierarchies, systems, and forms 2. The magnificence of existence is valued over material possessions 3. Flexibility, spontaneity, and functionality have the highest priority 4. Differences can be integrated into interdependent, natural flows 5. Understands that chaos and change are natural	Informational planetary global	Vision logic	
	Turquoise/ Holistic	Experience the wholeness of existence through mind and spirit	30	1. The world is a single, dynamic organism with its own collective mind 2. Self is both distinct and a blended part of a larger, compassionate whole 3. Everything connects to everything else in ecological alignments 4. Energy and information permeate the Earth's total environment 5. Holistic, intuitive thinking and cooperative actions are to be expected			Self-transcendence

Table 1: Growth Levels for Values, Major Epochs, Cognition, and Needs

There is a correlation between the Major Epochs and values. Basic themes for each value are given in Table 1, column 3. Foraging tribes are associated with beige and purple values. The basic theme of beige may be characterized as "Do what you must just to stay alive," and, for purple, it may be stated as "Keep the spirits happy and the tribe's nest warm and safe." The organized hunt is associated with the red meme, whose theme is "Be what you are and do what you want, regardless." The horticultural (use of the hoe) village is at the beginning of the blue meme. Later on, states with blue values developed as agrarian (use of the plow) economic production became the primary technology used. The basic theme is "Life has meaning, direction, and purpose with predetermined outcomes." Industrialization did not become dominant until the late nineteenth century as orange values, summarized as "Act in your own self-interest by playing the game to win," began to come to the fore. The information age has now exploded upon us, and this brings us to green, yellow, and turquoise values. Green's theme is "Seek peace within the inner self and explore, with others, the caring dimensions of community." "Live fully and responsibly as what you are and learn to become" and "Experience the wholeness of existence through mind and spirit" are basic themes of yellow and turquoise values, respectively. See Table 1, column 5, for five basic values associated with each meme that will be used throughout the book. Column 4 lists how many years ago the values associated with each theme began to develop. In his book, *Integral Psychology*, which was published in 2000, Wilber estimated that of the world's adult population, roughly 40% has blue, 30% has orange, and 10% green or higher values.[13] He estimated, in 2011,[14] that possibly 4% of the population has moved to the second-tier memes of yellow and turquoise, whereas, in 2000, he estimated that total at 1%.[15]

Each successive level becomes more complex as it develops. Wilber suggests that if 10% of the population reaches the second-tier yellow and turquoise levels, it will have a very significant effect on the culture at large because more-complex levels of values can have more power than their percentage of the population would indicate. For example, he estimates that the orange meme, with only 30% of the population, has 50% of the power, and green has 10% of the population and 15% of the power.[16]

The number of years associated with each meme is the estimated amount of time that these values have been present for a significant portion of humanity. But the less-complex values are also parts of our lives. And so, everyone with a dominant center of gravity in one valueMEME also has incorporated the less-complex values at some point in their lives. In fact, as children grow up, they usually go through the different value stages from Instinctive/Survivalistic to Magical/Animistic to Impulsive Egocentric to Purposeful/Authoritarian by around age 14. An example of the incorporation of a less-complex value system would be organized sports, like football, which offer a fairly healthy way for most people to express their red values of "Conquers, outfoxes, and dominates other aggressive characters" but with rules centered in blue values.

How do the valueMEME characteristics apply to economics beyond the technology associated with them? While gangs, including the mafia, do not participate in organized hunts, their values are red and purple (dominantly red, but with purple influence as well). Two values from Table 1 associated with red are "Stands tall, expects attention, demands respect, and calls the shots" and "Conquers, outfoxes, and dominates other aggressive characters." And in running the underground economy with illegal activities such as gambling, prostitution, and drugs, this characteristic stands out: "Enjoys self to fullest right now without guilt or remorse."

Less than 2% of the population[17] has jobs in farming in the United States, but a large portion of its population has blue values that have carried over from before the Industrial Revolution when a majority of the population was engaged in agriculture. This is not too surprising since those values have been around for 5,000 years. Take the first characteristic in Table 1 for the blue meme, "One sacrifices self to the transcendent Cause, Truth, or righteous Pathway." Regarding economics, it would not be surprising that people with these values would "buy American" to support our Christian country even though a foreign product might be the best product for the money.

The main theme of orange values is, "Act in your own self-interest by playing the game to win." This is a dominant value of capitalism and is associated with industrialization as the prevailing technology. This idea fits perfectly with free market economic theory, which holds that when all act in their own self-interest, things will work out the best for everyone.

The next valueMEME of green responds by saying, "Feelings, sensitivity, and caring supersede cold rationality." This leads us to the passage of laws to regulate the problems of capitalism through the development of welfare, unemployment compensation, government-funded retirement programs such as Social Security in the United States, and environmental and safety regulations. Mainstream economics admits the shortcomings of the free market system, with environmental economics and the study of poverty being major branches of the field. And half of the discipline is related to macroeconomics, which deals primarily with the instability of the business cycle. Much of the study of macroeconomics is devoted to how government can step in to control inflation and reduce unemployment. But orange-valued economists argue that government interference in the economy is unneeded when the economy goes into recession or there is instability in prices. They say such events keep the economy from naturally adjusting to full-employment levels.

Most arguments among economists in developed countries today are probably between those with orange and green values. The ones with green values emphasize the shortcomings of the free market system, and the orange-valued economists contend that the free enterprise system could solve all economic problems if the government would not interfere in markets. People with blue values in developed countries seem more likely to support the free market, except possibly when free trade is involved. They would be more likely to want their country's jobs protected. They are not as inclined to take a global viewpoint, which begins with the orange valueMEME. As cited previously, one characteristic of people with blue values is, "One sacrifices self to transcendent Cause, Truth, or righteous Pathway." The transcendent cause is usually their religion, whether it is Christianity, Islam, Buddhism, or another faith. They are also very nationalistic. And people with blue values support their own country's economic system, and in developed countries this is capitalism. In this case, in developed countries, the "transcendent cause" is free enterprise.

People with green values buy more expensive fuel-efficient cars and organic food to save the environment, and as previously mentioned, those with blue values support the idea that one should "buy American." You could say that both the blue- and green-valued consumers are possibly acting in their own self-interest in the long term. But this is different from a person with orange-centered values obtaining the best-valued good or service for their money and believing that everything will work out for the best economically by their doing so.

The values discussed so far are considered "subsistence" memes, but what about the second-tier "being" memes (see column 1 of Table 1)? The distinction between "being", as opposed to "subsistence," is relevant to economics. Take the yellow value: "The magnificence of existence is valued over material possessions." What does that say about economics? And the turquoise value, "Self is both distinct and a blended part of a larger, compassionate whole," certainly puts a different twist on self-interest.

Some economics professors even will take self-interest to an extreme, saying greed works out for everyone, especially those with orange values. And this is reflected in some of the attitudes of people in business because they are required to take economics courses in college to obtain a business degree. This is the Merriam-Webster definition of greed: "A selfish and excessive desire for more of something (such as money) than is needed."[18] Let us use the "excessive" and the "more of something (such as money) than is needed," parts of the definition and call greed excessive self-interest. Put this in juxtaposition to what the father of economics, Adam Smith, said: "It is not from the benevolence of the butcher, the brewer, or the baker that we expect our dinner, but from their regard for their own interest."[19] The problem is that self-interest can devolve into greed, and people are less likely to think twice about it, especially when economics professors are saying it will all work out okay. Our financial institutions' excessive selling of subprime loans to people who could not afford them was greed, as opposed to Adam Smith's idea of self-interest as a way of making a living. The sellers of these bad loans thought they could always foreclose if the customers could not pay, and this worked for the lenders as long as housing values kept going up. But it also led to the almost complete collapse of the world economy, and the most severe recession since the Great Depression. Some free-market advocates have tried to push the blame onto the government, saying that it encouraged the banks to make these loans. But the government did not require the banks to make subprime loans, and the credit unions did not do so. And not all banks were involved in subprime mortgages. The causes of the 1929 stock market crash that led to the Great Depression can also be put in the greed category. People took excessive risks by buying stock on margin, assuming it was easy money. And the stock market bubbles such as those in tech stocks, oil, and subprime mortgages can really be attributed to greed. To see the other end of greed on the self-interest spectrum, look at the turquoise value: "Self is both distinct and a blended part of a larger, compassionate whole." A person with this value would most likely act quite differently in making economic choices.

So, what proof that greed works out economically do some economists present? They often present the economic model of perfect competition. Perfect competition is characterized by thousands of small sellers, none of which can have any impact on price. And in this case, producers tend to produce at the minimum point of the long-run average cost (LRAC) curve, resulting in no resource misallocation. Retired economics professor Dr. Werner Sichel of Western Michigan University was of the opinion that almost every industry has only a small number of sellers when geographic and definitional factors are considered. Look at almost any business, and it has only a few competitors, usually due to geographic factors. There are thousands of supermarkets in the United States, so there are lots of sellers. Of course, who is going to drive to the next state to buy groceries, or even very far from where they live? In effect, the grocery store consumer has only a few supermarkets that are within a few miles of their house when they decide to buy groceries. But you can take almost any industry except farming and see each has only a few competitors when geographic or practical factors are accounted for. This market structure with a few sellers is called oligopoly by economists and is shown by economic theory to charge higher prices and produce less output than if there were thousands of sellers. But large oligopoly firms can have economies of scale that keep prices low. These can be realized when companies can lower costs through quantity discounts from buying in bulk and are able to use larger, more efficient plants and machinery. Hence, they can keep prices lower, possibly offsetting the higher prices that would be charged due to reduced competition when there is a small number of firms. This is evidenced by new industries as their product comes into common use. You have fewer companies manufacturing personal computers than when they first came out, and lower prices. But what about when this industry matures, and the few sellers remaining have little competition? Miller says, "All in all, there is no definite evidence of serious resource misallocation in the United States because of oligopolies."[20] But this also means that there really is "no definite evidence" that there is not. Therefore, Miller's argument that it works out economically for the best when everyone acts in their own self-interest, let alone greedily, is actually weak. In fact, economic theory says currently oligopolistic businesses do not allocate resources efficiently since they do not produce at the minimum point of the LRAC curve. This will be discussed in more detail in the Minimizing Costs section of Chapter 4.

3. Cognition

Look at the Cognition column in Table 1. It will help us talk about how people think at various levels. The differences may be related to education, the rationality assumption of economists, and the way people think at different levels relating to education and economic development. The modes of cognition are developed extensively in Ken Wilber's book *Sex, Ecology and Spirituality,* but only short summaries of them will be given here. Note that the levels of development for cognition and values discussed here are just two of many lines of development. Other lines that have been studied include morals, music, and needs. Wilber talks about cognition and the development of all other lines. "A major reason that the cognitive line is necessary and not sufficient for the other lines is that you have to be aware of something in order to act on it, feel it, identify with it, or need it."[21] This means that someone may be able to cognize at a certain level before that person can have orange values. But, according to Wilber, such a person might be able to think rationally, which is usually associated with the orange meme but still have blue or less-complex values. Osama Bin Laden and Al Qaeda would be good examples of this. They were capable of thinking at the rational orange level, by using science to come up with a way to destroy the World Trade Center, but their values were blue as they were dedicated to the "transcendent cause" of Islam.

The cognitive levels and their correspondence with Spiral Dynamics values will now be examined. "Preoperational thinking is, for cognitive anthropologists, thinking that works with images, symbols, and concepts (but not complex rules and operations)."[22] This idea corresponds to the purple and red value levels.

The concrete operational mind that corresponds with blue meme values can handle complex rules and operations but is still a "subject trying to look at and understand and operate on a world of objects."[23] This brings us to formal operational thought, which corresponds to orange values. Cognitive psychologists and anthropologists consider the formal operational level as corresponding to rational thought. And this "means the capacity not just to think, but to think about thinking."[24] The next level of thought is vision logic, which is defined as "the mind looking at the mind intersubjectively."[25] That is what we are trying to do here. We are looking at how a mind thinks at different levels of the lines of development. A person has progressed cognitively because they can now take the perspective that recognizes that they can think rationally. And they realize that rationality at the orange level has its limits. They see, for example, that businesses, applying their rational self-interest of maximizing profits, often ignore the environmental impact, which imposes external costs that are not accounted for. This will be discussed more extensively in the next section. The yellow and turquoise "being" memes correspond to the psychic level of cognition. Here, the turquoise value and level of cognition are quite similar. People with this value view the world in this way: "Self is both distinct and a blended part of a larger, compassionate whole."

4. Rationality

Table 1 includes rough estimates of the years that a significant portion of the population has had those values and the corresponding levels of cognition. Very small segments of the population would think in these ways during previous eras of human history. For example, formal operational (rational) thought is related to the orange meme. This did not become a dominant mode of thought in a significant segment of the population until the Age of Enlightenment, but it was talked about in Aristotle's philosophy in the fourth century B.C. But only a very small segment of the population thought rationally then.

What about the rationality assumption in economics? The examples used will be similar to those used for self-interest. Ken Wilber says, "The word rational is an impossible label; it means a million things to a million people."[26] But Roger Miller's version of the rationality assumption as it appears in his textbook, "We assume that individuals do not intentionally make decisions that would leave themselves worse off,"[27] is not what most people would think of when talking about rationality. This relates to self-interest more than rationality. Miller does go on to say that behavioral economists have come up with a theory of bounded rationality that "suggest[s] that traditional economic models assume that people exhibit three 'unrealistic' characteristics:

1. *Unbounded selfishness.* People are interested only in their own satisfaction.
2. *Unbounded willpower.* Their choices are always consistent with their long-term goals.
3. *Unbounded rationality.* They are able to consider every relevant choice.[28]

So, the rationality assumption already has its critics within the ranks of behavioral economists. Let us see what else Wilber says: "Weber, for example, differentiated between purposive rationality (such as scientific-technological knowledge), formal rationality (such as mathematics), and intersubjective or practical rationality (as displayed in morals or communication)."[29] Economists are trying to talk about purposive and formal rationality. They try to stay with positive economics, and this would usually mean something that can be measured. One example is that economists say the consumer will buy the best-valued product or service they can afford, given their budget. But, as stated previously, someone with blue values might decide to "buy American" to support US jobs even though a foreign product may be the best-valued product. And green-valued people may buy more expensive organic food to help the environment. The examples just cited that use Spiral Dynamics valueMEMES would support the unbounded selfishness criticism of the behavioral economists. So, when we take someone's values into account, we know for sure only that the 30% of the population in the orange meme are acting rationally in consumer decisions. But more could be acting rationally by buying the best-valued product because of budget constraints or convenience. Someone with blue values may want to "buy American," or someone with green values may want to purchase the more expensive better-mileage car but decide they cannot afford its higher price. And organic food is more difficult to obtain in less populated areas.

One more point Wilber makes concerns a prerational/transrational fallacy.[30] Sometimes people are confused because they conflate all irrational decisions. A person who cannot think rationally may make the irrational decision of not buying the best-valued product because of this. But someone who is transrational knows what the best product for their money is, but chooses to purchase something else that is better for the environment due to their green or more-complex values.

5. Needs and Wants

Let us examine the definition of economics used previously: "The study of how people allocate their scarce resources to satisfy their unlimited wants."[31] The key parts of this definition are "scarce resources" and "unlimited wants." Are resources limited, or scarce? If you use the definition of scarcity that some economists use, "A situation in which the ingredients for producing the things that people desire are insufficient to satisfy all wants at a zero price,"[32] then they are. But, as Louise Hay wrote, "Your prosperity consciousness is not dependent on money; your flow of money is dependent upon your prosperity consciousness. As you conceive of more, more will come into your life."[33] Is it as simple as thinking positively in this way? It is more complicated, but it is time, from an overall evolutionary perspective to think resources are abundant. Technology is advancing at an ever-more rapid rate, so more goods can be produced more efficiently, and as countries develop to incorporate orange values, population growth declines. Less-developed countries went from a fertility rate of 6.06 to 2.65 between 1950 and 2015, but, in the least-developed regions, the decline was only from 6.58 to 4.30.[34] China's one-child policy may be too extreme a way of dealing with high fertility rates, for the decline appears to happen naturally as countries progress. Most industrialized countries have on average smaller families than less-developed ones. The 2015 fertility rate for industrialized countries was 1.67 in 2015.[35]

And there is the idea of the Singularity:

Abstract: Ray Kurzweil and others have posited that the confluence of nanotechnology, artificial intelligence, robotics, and genetic engineering will soon produce posthuman beings that will far surpass us in power and intelligence. Just as black holes constitute a "singularity" from which no information can escape, posthumans will constitute a "singularity" whose aims and capacities lie beyond our ken. I argue that technological posthumanists, whether wittingly or unwittingly, draw upon long-standing Christian discourse of "theosis," according to which humans are capable of being God or god-like. From St. Paul and Luther to Hegel and Kurzweil, the idea of human self-deification plays a prominent role. Hegel in particular emphasizes that God becomes wholly actualized only in the process by which humanity achieves absolute consciousness. Kurzweil agrees that God becomes fully actual only through historical processes that illuminate and thus transform the entire universe.[36]

Essentially, this is saying that as technological change occurs at an ever-increasing rate, and humans correspondingly increase their level of consciousness, they become transformed into higher beings. Supporting this are the Table 1 time frames for the different Spiral Dynamics values stages, which have decreased at an ever-faster rate. Going from the beginning of blue to orange took 4,700 years, and from orange to green 150 years. Going from green to yellow took 100 years, and yellow to turquoise 20 years. The time estimates for the singularity occurring have ranged from now until after 2100.

Think about what is happening now with smartphones, iPads, and quick access to information. We are more and more able to see any movie, read any book, communicate with anyone on the planet, and listen to any music we wish. Although implanting a computer chip that is connected to your brain so that you can do this makes one feel uneasy, people have pacemakers and

other medical devices put inside them now. And how out of the realm of possibility is the next step that allows you to simply do all of this without any
electronic device at all? Essentially this is extra-sensory perception as the
dominant mode of communication. And technology will also continue to deal
with material needs as well. So, start thinking of abundance instead of scarcity
when it comes to economics and that technology seems to be making it happen
anyway.

The existing economic theory of supply and demand also contradicts the
idea of scarcity. The idea of peak oil that says we will run out of oil has been
contradicted by the working of supply and demand twice in the last forty
years. When the peak oil idea was broached during the oil crisis of the 1970s,
by a student in Dr. Myron Ross' economics class at Western Michigan University, he asked the question "At what price?" His argument was that as supply
decreases, prices would go up to the point where oil would not be depleted.
It would just be more expensive. And the quantity supplied increased as it
became feasible to pursue more expensive oil through offshore drilling and
other means, and the demand decreased due to more fuel-efficient cars and
other energy-saving devices until prices collapsed in the late 1980s. We saw
this again as more expensive oil prices made its extraction through the fracking process financially viable, causing the quantity supplied to increase, while
car fuel efficiency improved, decreasing demand. As a result, prices came
down dramatically again. The Great Recession dramatically reduced demand,
but even as economies recovered, oil prices have not gone back to the $4/gal-
lon level of the early part of this century until recently. So, the peak oil theory,
or scarcity, has once again been disproved by economic supply-and-demand
theory. On the other hand, this line of reasoning ignores the environmental
risks of offshore drilling and fracking.

What about unlimited wants? Economics contradicts itself now by also
saying that people eventually have enough of any particular good, and more
becomes an economic bad. How many cars can most of us have before we have
no room to store, or possibly even use, them? And you see the super-rich starting foundations when they realize they have more than enough money than the
middle class and the less rich, and so donate to charities.

And what is behind the unlimited wants? It may be fear that there will not be enough money or goods (scarcity), or simply wanting the status money confers. These motivations are reflected in the orange value, which holds that "Optimistic, risk-taking, and self-reliant people deserve success." So, large homes and high income validate their success. The first issue is dealt with by thinking abundantly. This may seem contradictory, but thinking abundantly does not mean there will be excessive displays of wealth for everyone, but that there will be plenty of resources to live well if you think positively about it. And look at the green value: "The human spirit must be freed from greed, dogma, and divisiveness." So, people with green values are already recognizing the problem of greed, or the fear of there not being enough for everyone. What about the status issue? One of the ideas held by those with yellow values is that "The magnificence of existence is valued over material possessions." As more and more people evolve to these types of values, this would certainly put a limit on wants of a material nature. But what is behind the whole idea of evolution itself? In a way, it is unlimited wants. It is really a need to continue to create more of the Good, the True, and the Beautiful. And if we are thinking abundantly, is there any limit to this? So, the economic problem now becomes one of how we encourage thinking about abundance instead of scarcity. Is this easy? No, because most of the world is thinking in terms of limited resources. The beige through green valueMEMES are called the "subsistence" memes. Even those with green values who recognize the problem with greed may see it more in terms of others wanting more than they need. Or even if they may not think greed is the issue, they see the solution to income inequality as redistributing income from the rich to the poor through welfare programs and/or a progressive income tax. While redistributing income has its place, this is still thinking of scarcity instead of abundance for all. The yellow and turquoise valueMEMES are the "being" ones, and Ken Wilber estimates that with less than 10% of the population having those values, there are not enough people to begin to make a significant impact yet. But this is the direction in which we are evolving. And so, one economic problem should be how to get people thinking about abundance instead of scarcity. So, Louise Hay, by selling thirty-five million copies of her book *You Can Heal Your Life,* may be currently doing quite a bit to improve economic reality. And she is not just talking about abundance in money; she is talking about all areas of life including relationships, work, and physical and emotional well-being. This also relates to the evolutionary impulse.

So, if we take out the scarcity and unlimited wants, we could use Rudolf Steiner's definition: "The business of this economic life is to deal with whatever is production of commodities, circulation of commodities, consumption of commodities."[37]

Related to this definition is the question of whether all products and services will be produced and provided by robots in the future. So far new jobs have replaced the older jobs as technology developed. Manufacturing jobs replaced farming ones. There were no information technology occupations eighty years ago. Some have said this is changing, and that current jobs are not being replaced at a sufficient rate as technology advances.[38] If this happens, some form of guaranteed income may need to be implemented, and one's purpose in life may need to be reconsidered.

a. Hierarchy of Needs

Related to the values memes of Spiral Dynamics is Abraham Maslow's Hierarchy of Needs, and these have a separate column in Table 1. The placement on the table is from Wilber's book *Integral Psychology*.[39] Roger Miller in his textbook, *Economics Today,* makes this statement: "Indeed, from the economist's point of view, the term *needs* is objectively undefinable."[40] The fact that we talk about poverty and unemployment rates in economics would contradict this statement. What else could these economic measures reflect but needs? But the needs are relative to the values. Physiological needs relate to beige values. Safety needs correspond to red values and belongingness to blue values. The self-esteem and self-actualization needs are relevant to the orange and green memes. Lastly, the self-transcendence need would correspond to yellow and turquoise values. One might say, of course, that these psychological needs are quite different from what most people think about when talking about "needs" in economics. People usually think only of physiological needs such as air, food, water, shelter, etc. One could say this is really not an economic issue, but there are studies documenting that losing a job can cause psychological problems:

Covariance analyses adjusted for background variables support findings from earlier studies that long-term unemployment and perceived job insecurity are detrimental: short-term unemployed and secure permanent employees experienced fewer psychological complaints and lower subjective complaints load, reported a higher self-rated health, and were more satisfied with their life compared to long-term unemployed and insecure permanent employees.[41]

This relates to the self-esteem need, and Maslow's Hierarchy of Needs can definitely be of value when talking about economics.

b. Technology and Needs

Needs are relative to the technology of a society as well. Bows and arrows, or spears, are needed in hunting and food-gathering societies. In agricultural societies, a plow and animals to pull it are necessary. Transportation is usually needed in an industrial society. If a city does not have good mass transit, such as in Detroit, Michigan's metropolitan area, an automobile is probably necessary to travel to work or buy physical goods, or mass transit needs to be improved. Since southeast Michigan is the car capital of the world, leaders in Detroit have provided a good expressway system as an alternative to mass transportation. In the information age, access to the Internet is needed. That is why there is a strong argument for designating cable Internet services as a public utility in the United States. And that is why electricity and telephone services have been, or are, considered public utilities. But in a purposive world, the need to regulate this could go away since public utilities already pay their employees a living wage, and their prices are relatively low. Covering the external costs of pollution would still be needed, especially with providers of electricity. Current economic theory indicates that public utilities are natural monopolies and should be allowed to earn a "normal" profit. Having economic entities voluntarily earn a "normal" profit will be talked about in more detail in the next section. Since all companies would be minimizing cost rather than maximizing profit, the need to regulate natural monopolies would most likely be less necessary.

This brings into question the near monopolies that have sprung up in the information age, such as Microsoft Windows and Facebook. Should they be regulated? An answer to this question could rest on whether or not the service they provide is a need. Possibly Facebook could be argued not to be necessary in today's world.

B. New Solutions

1. Purposive Economics

Economics talks about the production possibilities curve. It groups all goods and services into generalized categories, such as consumption goods and military goods. Consumption goods are those bought by consumers. It then graphs a hypothetical curve, with consumption goods and military goods measured on various axes, as illustrated in Figure 3.

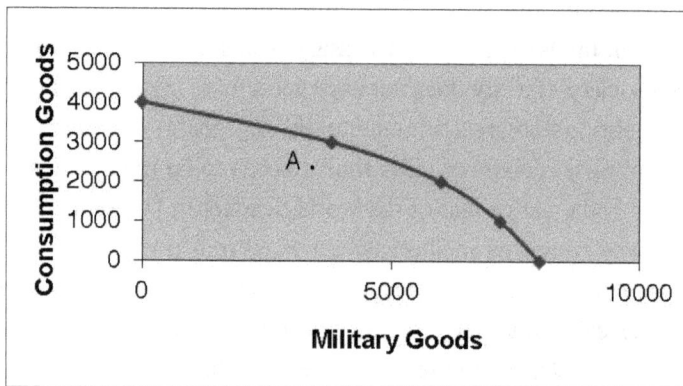

Figure 3: Production Possibilities Curve.

This curve represents all the different combinations of goods and services current technology can potentially produce if all resources are currently in use. So, at different points on the curve, you would have to give up making consumption goods to produce more military goods and vice versa. Then a point is put on the graph that is between the curve and the intersection of the axis, such as point A in Figure 3. This is to illustrate a hypothetical case where there is the unemployment of current resources, with the result that the economy is producing fewer goods than is possible at the current time. This is one of the major problems of the current capitalist economy. And it is somewhat accepted as just how it is. It is called the business cycle and assumes that every so often the economy will have periods of unemployment. But it does not have to be that way: communist countries simply mandate that everyone be employed, and they have fewer offices and factories standing empty and very little unemployment.

A comparison of the advantages and disadvantages of the managed, or socialist, and free market, or capitalist, economic systems used to be made in every introductory economics textbook. But since few communist countries remain, a comparison of managed and free market economies is often not presented. Therefore, recessions are pretty much accepted as inevitable. Or it is thought that capitalism has won, and it is the perfect economic system. But capitalism still has its disadvantages, as the Great Recession clearly demonstrated to us once again. Besides there being a business cycle with recessions and depressions, the current economic system assumes the person with more money is the better person; it treats people as objects; it can ignore the social costs of pollution; there is significant and growing income inequality, and businesses can forget their purpose of providing a good product or service at a reasonable price. All of this relates to maximizing profits.

The maximizing profit motive leads to some of the ways we treat people as objects by having human "resource" departments, writing about people as "inputs" in labor economic theory, and talking about "selling oneself." This supports the idea that the person making the highest income is the best person. The "input" that helps you best maximize profits is the most valuable for this goal, but this has little relation to how conscious, or moral, the person is. Such ideas also lead to income inequality and working excessive hours at the expense of one's mental health and family life, as people strive to prove they are the most valuable or "best" person.

External costs are often ignored by today's capitalist enterprises. And advertising to increase demand to earn more profits, as opposed to presenting information so that people are aware that your product or service exists and what it does, leads to overproduction of some products. This wastes resources and can create additional pollution.

Socialism also has its problems in that it can be inefficient or choose the wrong products or services to produce. Capitalism seems to be the better economic system so far, and it has been tremendous at stimulating technological advances and creating a middle class. And it would still have a place in economic development in countries where there are enough people with orange values to move to healthy industrialization, as evidenced by the success of countries in Asia, such as South Korea and China.

While capitalism has done many positive things economically in industrialized countries, it may well not be what is needed for the information age. And there are significant unconscious and conscious orange values in play, especially in the United States, that consider capitalism to be the solution to all our problems. Despite the problems already listed regarding capitalism, some economists call for very minimal regulation, and such arguments ignore the fundamental free market law that competition is better for the system than monopoly or oligopoly markets. There are tendencies, in some industries at least, toward monopolization. The extreme belief in capitalism can also lead its adherents to ignore evidence of the problems of pollution for the planet.

A possible solution to help moderate the business cycle, and address the other problems of capitalism, is proposed here. It does not discard the idea of a free market. The solution would involve a voluntary and gradual switch to purposive enterprises that are possibly owned by the employees and changes banking, educational, and medical institutions in the direction of customer-owned cooperatives. The government would not be involved except to provide vouchers for education, and possibly healthcare. The government would also still be involved in pollution control since its mission entails a concern for the whole, and it could come up with standards of allowable pollution that would not impact citizens' overall health. This actually could lower economic organization costs since some level of discharge of chemicals or gases into the environment may not impose any external costs. For instance, emissions in a small town in Wyoming might not have a significant negative impact on the environment.

It is proposed here that producers of goods and services follow a business model called purposive enterprise. They would dwell on their purpose as opposed to maximizing profits. Their goal would be to provide the best product or service they can at an affordable price. If a business goes to this model, it might improve its product quality or lower its costs if they already exist. Or if they are new producers, they would not provide inferior products or services just to make a profit. For example, if a new or existing economic organization could make a profit off a home loan, they would not do so knowing that the customer was unlikely to be able to afford it and that the house would have to be sold to recover their money.

Working at one's purpose in life should provide more satisfaction to people and this would also be a complementary goal of a purposive enterprise. So, people would be working, and this would include those doing nonpaid work at home, at something that is their purpose, rather than what makes them the most money or fame. So, a person might become an electronic technician as opposed to being a doctor if that is their true purpose in life. And a person whose occupation is, for example, that of an accountant, could work at an economic organization that provides a product or service they consider useful to society. They might have a job at a fast-food restaurant that provides nutritious food as opposed to one that makes products that are bad for people's health.

Instead of maximizing profits as they do now, businesses would just cover costs, including what economists call a normal profit. "Normal profit occurs when the difference between a company's total revenue and combined explicit and implicit costs are equal to zero."[42] Explicit costs are "Costs that business managers must take account of because they must be paid."[43] Implicit costs are "Expenses that managers do not have to pay out of pocket and hence normally do not explicitly calculate, such as the opportunity cost of factors of production that are owned. Examples are owner-provided capital and owner-provided labor."[44] So, accountants and the general population usually think of profits as revenue minus explicit costs. Accountants would call this net profit margin. A website analyzing S& P 500 constituents from 2001 to 2020 says, "Over this entire time period, the average net profit margin of the medians by year was 8.9%. So, we can surmise that a good net profit margin is 10% or above . . ."[45] A 20-year median for net profit margin seems to be a good way to approximate what a normal profit should be. So, for a purposive enterprise, the organization would keep its profits around 10% or less, and dwell more on its purpose rather than profits.

Another goal of a purposive economic entity is being aware of the external costs of pollution their product or production facility might generate and would be part of covering their costs and providing a quality product. Also related to covering costs would be the provision of a living wage to employees. This would not just involve subsistence-level wages, but also a chance to live quite comfortably, as the idea of abundance is embraced.

A living wage would help keep employees with orange or less-complex values from undermining a purposive enterprise as long as they live well. But a tiered wage structure might be needed until employees evolve to a degree where their income level ceases to be an important value. Volunteers and student employees might be an exception to the living wage goal if they are not concerned with currently making a living. And if the industry is a low-wage one, competition might force a lower wage, at least initially. But since there would be only normal profits at purposive organizations, any economic profits could go toward paying higher wages to staff. They could also go toward covering external costs, but there would be a conflict between increasing employees' incomes and paying for external costs or keeping prices low. A normal profit would be a maximum of 10%. If profits are above this level, the money could go toward reducing external costs, paying all employees a living wage, improving product quality, or reducing prices.

Dr. Amy K. Glasmeier of MIT first developed the Living Wage Calculator in 2004.[46] It is available at the county and metropolitan statistical area (a multicounty area surrounding a major city in the United States) levels. The Living Wage Calculator helps account for the large differences in cost of living, especially for housing, in different geographic areas. The calculator posits an hourly wage for eleven different family types from zero to three children and for one or two adults, whether one or both are working, and if one is working. It is given by the hour to make comparisons easier. An example of one family type for Washtenaw County, Michigan, would be that two adults, with one working full-time and three children, has a calculated living wage of $28.11/hour. The calculator also gives the poverty-level wage as $13/hour. The living wage for a single adult is $12.39/hour. This calls into question whether economic organizations could pay different wages for different family circumstances since there is a $15.72 difference between the two living wage examples given. Current thinking may probably say no, but each economic entity could possibly decide for itself. Or possibly the rights sector of a Threefold State that will be proposed in the next section could make this decision. And possibly this would be more of a concern when a very high percentage of the population has yellow and turquoise values, and/or scarcity and status issues are less pronounced as the economy becomes more stable with a high percentage of purposive enterprises. Overall wages do not need to be perfectly equal as long as everyone is at least making a living wage, and income disparities are not extreme.

This is a summary of the five basic principles that would guide a purposive enterprise:

1. Working at a job that is your purpose
2. Emphasis on the product or service
3. Covering costs as opposed to maximizing profits
4. Do no harm to the environment
5. Living wage

What about converting existing profit-maximizing companies into purposive organizations? Owners/shareholders may need to be bought out, and some owners of private companies might simply convert such companies because of their green, yellow, or turquoise values. Another possible alternative would involve employees or unions buying the company out. Credit unions for unions could possibly help with borrowing funds to buy out the current owners. Or people starting new economic entities could decide to make it a purposive one.

Competitors who remain profit-maximizing might complain of unfair competition. They could be forced through competition to embrace the proposed new type of economic enterprise or go out of business if one or more of their competitors are purposive and charge lower prices. This could accelerate the move to the new economy. This has already started: a majority of states have already passed laws allowing alternative types of corporations that are not required to maximize profits.

> The new laws permit companies to join the profit motive with the purpose of making a "positive impact on society and the environment." In their articles of incorporation, Benefit Corporations declare their public missions—things like bringing a local river back to life, providing affordable housing, facilitating animal adoptions or promoting adult literacy.[47]

So far, thirty-four states and the District of Columbia allow Benefit Corporations.[48]

The idea of gradually converting all organizations to purposive enterprises is a good alternative to socialism and profit-maximizing capitalism and can lead to less government regulation. People would be free to try to implement their ideas without the obstacles of government interference, bureaucracy, or the public sector taking on the task of figuring out what new product/service ideas are the best for the economy. Not all ideas for products or services would work out, of course, and a company's purpose might become no longer relevant, such as when video rental stores became obsolete. So, some organizations would cease to exist as they may no longer be needed, and others would never really succeed, to begin with, just as happens today with business failures. But instability is a major problem of capitalism, as self-interest devolves into greed in one or more markets and then periodically causes the economy to crash. This would probably be much less likely in an economy using a purposive enterprise model. The stock market and its boom-and-bust cycles would moderate since speculation would be reduced when people realize that profits would be at most 10%. So, gradually moving all private-sector economic enterprises to this model would hopefully cure or minimize the instability of capitalism, without the inefficiency of government regulation or ownership. But the new system would not be socialism since economic entities would still be in the private sector and compete in the market. So, the move to purposive enterprise could make both conservatives and liberals happy. The liberals would see less poverty due to unemployment and most, if not all employees earned a living wage. And there would be reduced pollution and slower climate change. And conservatives would see less regulation and taxes, making for a smaller government.

Purposive enterprise could create revenue problems for governments as the corporate income tax would be reduced, but as free enterprise advocates point out, only people can be taxed. Who really pays corporate income taxes? Is it the owners with lower profits, customers paying higher prices, or employees receiving lower wages? It is usually all three groups to some extent. So, would individuals and families be taxed more with the new breed of economic organization since there would be fewer profits to tax? Property taxes could still be charged to purposive enterprises since they need police, fire, and national defense protection. And government costs should be lowered due to less regulation being needed with economic organizations focused on providing the best product and service available as opposed to maximizing profits. And income-maintenance programs, such as unemployment and welfare, would be less expensive due to the business cycle being eliminated, or at least less pronounced, and the living wage goal would increase incomes. Therefore, it is plausible to expect that taxes on individuals would not increase and/or they could more easily pay them if their wages went up.

What would happen to technology growth with purposive enterprise? The hope of making large sums of money through patents is a major driver of innovation. Since a large portion of the population still has orange-free enterprise values, this would still be the primary mode of business for quite a while. But as economic entities evolve into this model, technological advancements could be continued as more and more individuals evolve and need self-actualization. Looking at Maslow's Hierarchy of Needs in Table 1, we can see that this need actually begins at the end of the orange meme, so it is important to many with green or more complex values. These people would not necessarily require the profit motive to create new technology but would do so out of this need. This would happen more and more often as people evolve to more complex green, yellow, and turquoise values.

What about consumer cooperatives as part of a new economy? Many nursery schools are operated as cooperatives. The New Morning School in the Detroit metropolitan area is an excellent nursery-through eighth-grade co-op school where parent participation is extensive. Such a model could be combined with voucher funding, or used for charter schools, where the state pays private schools the same amount public schools receive per pupil since a big problem at New Morning has been low teacher salaries. Most of the teachers in the co-op school have green values, and the job provides a second income for the families of many of them. But you know the teachers are there because they like the job. They are not primarily there for the money. And such motivations also contradict the traditional economic values of self-interest, which would hold that in order to obtain better teachers you need to pay a higher salary. So, for the most part, the teachers at this school reflect more complex than orange values, because having a job that satisfies them is more important than the money they earn. But the supply of teachers is also limited because, while others may want to teach at this school, they simply need to make more money to make a living, especially in a one-income family. The school is not a charter- or voucher-funded school but relies on tuition and fundraising, so this holds salaries down.

Anne Dwyer, who works on people using Muscle Activation Techniques, once said we should do healthcare instead of health insurance. This idea would correspond to the purposive enterprise principle of emphasizing the product rather than profits. Healthcare currently is influenced heavily by the government and by health insurance organizations. Blue Cross is nonprofit now but still thinks like a for-profit organization with orange values in many cases. A way to start emphasizing healthcare would be to set up cooperative customer-owned healthcare systems similar to cooperative schools. The buyers of healthcare would have a say in how it operates, as opposed to the government or the owners of the profit-minded healthcare businesses. A particular problem with the profit motive in the healthcare industry involves the issue of death and disability. Using demand and supply allows doctors, current healthcare businesses, medical equipment suppliers, and the pharmaceutical industry to charge exorbitant prices since a person's demand for a service that would save their life, or fix a severe disability, is often equal to someone's total wealth. Cooperative healthcare would help solve this demand issue for doctors and other healthcare providers, but not for the medical drug market or for durable and nondurable health products. But the costs should come down as these industries move to purposive enterprise. These cooperative health-care organizations would very likely grow out of the current hospital systems, the health insurance companies, or some combination thereof. Starting from scratch would be a very challenging task, so a gradual transition from profit-motivated, or even the current nonprofit ones that tend to act like for-profit organizations, to the purposive ideal would be the best way to proceed with this. The key difference would be that the customers could vote and run for the board, and possibly even be required to work a few hours a week at a healthcare facility similar to a co-op school. The buyer would be a much more educated consumer/owner as a result.

Related to this is the idea of social entrepreneurship. While there is dis-agreement on a definition of this idea, here is an attempt to define it:

> The social entrepreneur is a mission-driven individual who uses a set of entrepreneurial behaviors to deliver a social value to the less privileged, all through an entrepreneurially oriented entity that is financially independent, self-sufficient, or sustainable.[48]

So, this is close to being a purposive enterprise, but it still may rely on dona-tions or government funding. But there is an attempt to move away from these sources of income and be self-sustaining. And purposive enterprise would be for everyone, not just the less privileged.

But how will this be financed, as economist Milton Friedman of "there is no free lunch" fame would ask? Healthcare would be considered a right, so the government would step in, in this case by requiring everyone to have access to a hospital system. Some argue it is not a right, but every other developed coun-try in the world has universal healthcare, and even the United States passed the Affordable Care Act, which was a move to work toward covering the whole population. And even before it was passed, US hospitals provided for those without insurance through their emergency rooms and charged higher prices to their other customers who have health insurance or wealth sufficient to pay for the services.

Do you subsidize families or single individuals to join a healthcare system, provide it through the government, or require economic entities to provide their employees with healthcare? Currently, the Affordable Care Act uses all three methods of finance, but it is oriented toward health insurance. The government subsidizes low-income, disabled, and senior individuals, at least partially. The Affordable Care Act requires firms that have fifty or more employees who work at least thirty hours per week to provide insurance to these workers. The first and last methods of finance are controversial. Some say subsidizing people is too costly in terms of higher taxes on some. Employers who did not previously provide healthcare insurance are saying they cannot afford it or are changing employees' hours, or laying off or not hiring more individuals, to avoid the higher costs in an attempt to stay below government-mandated minimum levels for providing coverage.

A possible funding mechanism would be to have economic organizations provide a healthcare voucher to employees, including those who are working fewer or no hours because of disability. The government would subsidize employers who cannot afford to pay the vouchers until they are able to do so and would set the value of the vouchers. This would be the least disruptive way of financing since employers already provide healthcare insurance for a significant segment of the population now. Medicare would still provide for the retired and disabled, but healthcare costs should come down in the new economy. People without healthcare, becausee they are without a job, would be financed by the government, but this would be significantly less needed as unemployment declined. And food suppliers would be more concerned about quality food that does not cause health problems for consumers; for instance, they may not add sugar to their products to help reduce the number of people becoming diabetic. This would also lessen the need for healthcare services.

If a country is about to implement a universal healthcare system, a government-funded voucher system might be the best way to finance healthcare.

And credit unions came through the financial crisis well. A big reason is that they did not provide any subprime mortgages. They were concerned about making bad loans to their members. Could economic organizations not set up their own cooperatives for borrowing money? If credit unions are set up for economic entities and unions, this could make them less reliant on the stock market. There would also be no need for financial institutions to strive for unrealistic profit margins, or emphasize short-term gains at the expense of long-term stability, to keep their stock prices up. If all banking went to a co-op concept, this would cut down on bad loans as a major factor in contributing to recessions. Again, credit unions did not make these risky loans since they knew they were not good for their members. Cooperative lending organizations owned by their members are more likely to be concerned about the quality of their loans to owner-members whether the loans are for private individuals or economic institutions.

If you are self-employed, or in a partnership with no employees, simply make a living. Do not worry about whether you are making too much money unless you are ruining your health or family life by working too many hours. Do consider whether you are fulfilling your life's purpose and providing a useful product or service to society. But once you have employees, you should consider paying a living wage to them. Environmental concerns would be less likely to be a concern with a small organization but could be a problem with issues such as the aesthetics of a building you own, noise pollution, or not following zoning laws if working from home.

So, should producers of goods and services be required to be purposive enterprises, and should co-ops be mandated for banking, education, and healthcare? No, except possibly for healthcare and education since education is already accepted as a right, and the United States is the last developed country to start to see healthcare as one. For one thing, evolution seems a better policy than revolution. Radical change is too hard to assimilate; an example may be seen in the imposition of communism in every country it was tried. The American Revolution was a success because it restored what had already existed when the British government tried to exert more control. You must have enough people with cognition and values at the new level to evolve to it. Otherwise, revolutions aimed at radical change are doomed to fail, or simply replace the existing power structure with a similar one that in the end displays the same values as the previous one. This happened with revolutions in many Latin American countries. There is a small percentage of people with Spiral Dynamics second-tier values at present, and things will change rapidly enough because evolution seems to be moving faster and faster. It must, in order to keep up with the rapid technological changes we are seeing today.

2. Rudolf Steiner's Threefold State

Rudolf Steiner published a book that in one English translation from German was titled *The Threefold State: The True Aspect of the Social Question*. He wrote about history at the end of the eighteenth century, "'Fraternity! Equality! Liberty!'—these three words rang out as a motto of the new order."[49] But he also wrote that thinkers in the nineteenth century believed the three impulses were contradictory. For example, equality and liberty could be shown to be at odds. An example of this today would be those arguing they should have the "freedom" to refuse services to lesbian, gay, bisexual, and transgender (LGBT) people based on their religious beliefs although this is in opposition to "equality" for this group. Steiner also wrote that ". . . at the same time one's general human feeling must be in sympathy with all three ideals alike."[50] His solution to the problem was this:

> The reason why the contradiction arises is, that the three ideals only acquire their true social significance when we perceive that the body social has necessarily a threefold character. Its three branches must not be artificially centralized into some abstract theoretical kind of unity in a parliament or otherwise. They must become three actual, living members of the social body, each centered in itself, working alongside one another in cooperation.[51]

The three divisions of the social system would be the economy, the rights, and the individual/cultural sector. Fraternity is dealt with in the economy and deals with the production, circulation, and consumption of commodities. Steiner says that here men work together out of their common interest. The next part of the body social deals with equality, or human rights, and would be the concern of what is the public sector currently. And the third part of the body social "includes everything that rests upon the natural aptitudes of the private individual."[52] This is where freedom is allowed expression. It would include households, educational institutions, and spiritual organizations. This sector could be given responsibility for healthcare since it would be functioning similarly to education cooperatives. But lending institutions for economic entities or unions, even if organized as cooperatives, should still be in the economic sector since they are so important to that sector. Steiner did not say that healthcare or credit unions for families should be in the individual/cultural sector, but since it is being proposed that they be consumer-owned cooperatives, they would better fit there.

Steiner wrote that the three parts of the social order would act similarly to the way independent states do now. He writes, "The necessary transactions between the executive of the equity-state and the body economic will be carried on pretty much as those between the governments of sovereign States at present."[53] But he also says that "everything that in the economic sphere forms the basis of an equitable relationship between man and man, must in a healthy body social be regulated by the equity state."[54] So the rights of LGBT individuals would be current issues where the equity state could step in regarding economic life as far as guaranteeing nondiscrimination in employment, housing, and other areas. Steiner also advocated state expropriation of capital from current users and allocation of this to those who would be more productive. This would be similar to the government changing the composition of General Motors' executive staff in the automotive bailout, but this would be done by the governing body of the economic sector. This would possibly be a very rare occurrence due to competition and the emphasis on producing the best product or service possible for the lowest cost at purposive entities.

Steiner discusses how the state currently has too much influence on spiritual life:

> the practical requirements of the State give a certain stamp to men's thoughts, and that these requirements represent the requirements of the ruling classes. The working-class thinker saw in the life of thought a reflection of material interests and contending interests; and this aroused in him a feeling, that all spiritual life was ideology—a reflection of the economic order of the world.

> Man's spiritual life will cease to be rendered desolate by such a view, when it becomes possible to perceive that, in the domain of the mind and spirit, there reigns a reality that transcends material

external circumstance, and bears within itself its own matter and substance.[55]

He goes on to write, "Art, science, general philosophy, and all that is connected with these, have need of such an independent place within human society."[56] Hence he writes that schools should be taken out of the public sector. He suggests that economic organizations should pay employees with children extra to cover the educational costs of their children. But as stated previously, the growth of charter schools seems to show how education is moving toward the private sector now. The difference is that the money now comes from the public sector, and for practical reasons, this seems to be something that should not be changed since it would be too disruptive to the economic sector. He is also of the opinion that the move of education from the public to the private sector should be done gradually to avoid too much disruption. The move to charter schools should be evolutionary, or gradual, as well, which seems to be how it is proceeding currently in the United States. He also maintains that the judicial system should be in the spiritual sector, or

will be the separation of the magistracy from the institutions of the political state. The latter will have to define the rights that are to be recognized between men, or groups of men. But the actual decision of cases will come under institutions developed from within the spiritual state. The judgment passed is to a very great measure dependent on the judge's ability to have imagination and understanding for the individual circumstances of the person he is trying. Such imaginative understanding will only be present when those ties of sympathy and confidence which link individuals to institutions of the spiritual state are also made the determining element in the constitution of tribunals. Possibly the directing body of the spiritual state might make a panel of magistrates taken from the greatest possible variety of professions, who, after the expiration of a fixed period, would go back to their own callings.[57]

Steiner suggests terms of five to ten years for judges. This would truly make the judiciary less subject to politics, as it is supposed to be now. And it would solve the problem of people voting for judges when they have little idea of their merits, especially in lower courts.

Steiner provides support for other economic ideas suggested in this book so far. He talks about something similar to the development of cooperatives:

> The economic organization will encourage the formation of associations composed of men, who by their trade or as consumers, have the same interests, or whose wants in some other respect are similar; and these associations will mutually cooperate to carry on the whole business of the economic state.[58]

While not exactly advocating a 10% profit rule Steiner says profits should be reinvested, "so long he must be allowed to retain right of use over that sum total which has accrued to the initial capital as profits on the business,—provided always this increment is applied to the further development of the productive industry."[59] And in support of evolution rather than revolution: "To imagine that in twenty-four hours a transformation can be effected in public life, is recognized by prudent socialists themselves to be a delusion. They rather look to affect their regeneration of society through gradual and appropriate transformations."[60] And gradualism has already been suggested in connection with moving education out of the public sector.

Other economic issues are addressed in *The Threefold Social Order:*

> Similar to a child's right to education is the right of old people, invalids, widows, and sick persons to a maintenance. For this, capital will have to be forthcoming for the community's use, as in the case of the subsidy for the education of those who are not yet mature. The essential point of it all is, that the amount received by persons who are not themselves earning should not be a result of the economic life; but, conversely, that the economic life should depend on what the sense of right has to say in this connection. The workers in any

economic state will be able to keep less of the proceeds of their labor, the more is required for the non-producers.[61]

International relations would be threefold so that each sector could negotiate separately with the corresponding sector in another country. Steiner writes, "The result will be such an interweaving of interests of the various communities as will make frontiers seem negligible in the common life of mankind."[62] The European Union, and similar associations, are examples of this despite the countries not being threefold.

3

Resources and Supply and Demand

A. Resources

ECONOMICS CURRENTLY CONCEIVES of five resources, or factors of production, in the introductory chapters of the textbooks for its first-level college courses. These resources are land, labor, physical capital, human capital, and entrepreneurship. Land includes timber, minerals, fish, water, and the fertility of the soil. Labor comprises the people who work to produce goods and services. Physical capital consists of factories and machines, and improvements to the land, such as dams that are used to produce other products and services. The education and training of the workforce is human capital. And entrepreneurship is the part of labor that organizes, takes risks, and manages the other factors of production. The definition of resources in economics textbooks used to be broken up into just land, labor, and capital, and the last two resources listed could easily still be included under labor. These additions seem to emphasize orange values that champion capitalism. For example, take the value from Table 1: "Optimistic, risk-taking, and self-reliant people deserve success." This can be, and is, used to justify the extremely high incomes of some entrepreneurs, and making it a separate resource makes entrepreneurship more important. And it has been stated previously that this value has contributed to the great technological growth and prosperity that mankind has experienced in recent centuries. But it has also been written in this book previously that as people's values become more complex, this monetary motivation becomes less important. And "human capital" obviously emphasizes capitalism by the use of the last word in the phrase. It could just as easily be called education.

Looking at education another way, we have already discussed Ken Wilber's point that we probably need 10% of the population to be at second-tier values to make a difference in evolution. Wilber has detailed in *Integral Life Practice*, the book that he coauthored with Terry Patten, Adam Leonard, and Marco Morelli, how working on your cognition (mind), physical body, emotional life (shadow), and spirituality can accelerate development to increasing levels of consciousness.[63] So, such work would change existing ideas about education somewhat in its emphasis on emotional life and spirituality, as opposed to education's current emphasis on cognition almost exclusively.

It is currently talked about in economic theory that resources are scarce, as previously discussed. Take, for example, land. This scarcity may change when the population peaks. Developed countries do not have significant population growth, and as countries develop, they are starting to see their birth rates decline, as previously documented. But land may continue to be relatively "scarce" in densely populated areas. The scarcity of land in urban centers may become less important though. This would be due to increased acceptance of working from home, and more extensive use of the Internet and video-conferencing technologies. Still, the scarcity of land may remain an issue because of climate and beauty questions. More pleasant weather conditions and the natural beauty of being located by water or mountains would still make land more valuable in those areas. Location by water is important for the transportation of goods over water, and location by mountains and/or water is important for tourism reasons. And it has already been stated that the economic theory of supply and demand itself disputes the depletion of natural resources, such as oil. The idea of labor being scarce is contradicted by the prevalence of unemployment problems in developed and developing countries. And with capital, the problem of factories and office buildings sitting idle during recessions is similar to the labor problem in that scarcity is rarely the major problem in developed countries. In Chapters 5 and 6, this scarcity issue will be discussed in relation to the values of a culture. The development of co-op lending institutions could also help in relation to scarcity. And the idea of risk-taking on the part of an individual who wants to use their own money to start an economic entity could be covered by making a loan to the organization, and if there is a failure, the entrepreneur would be the first paid off from the assets remaining. This would lower the risk.

Pollution and climate change certainly are relevant to the scarcity-of-resources topic, but this will be covered in Chapter 6.

B. Supply and Demand

Following the introductory chapters in principles of economics courses, there are usually two chapters on the theory of supply and demand. They detail how supply and demand work in markets to determine both the price of goods and the quantities of goods to be produced. Converting economic entities to purposive ones would change existing ideas on supply and demand little. Their interaction would continue to work toward allocating resources, as opposed to the socialist idea of the government deciding how much to produce at what cost. A complete discussion of supply and demand theory will not be provided here since little of it would be changed by moving to purposive enterprise, but some issues relating to it will be discussed.

The idea of the government setting minimum and maximum prices in certain markets is discussed by economists when talking about supply and demand. They talk about price floors and price ceilings, and how shortages and surpluses are created when the government sets prices above or below the market level if the forces of supply and demand are not allowed to work. A price floor that is set above the market price causes surpluses to occur since suppliers produce more than buyers want at an artificially high level. Two areas where the government currently steps in to set price floors are agriculture and setting the minimum wage. Both of these markets are very competitive, with many suppliers providing the same product or service. In the case of the minimum wage, government regulations apply mainly to unskilled labor, as workers have no way to differentiate themselves other than showing how reliable they are. If the price of labor is set above the market rate, it can lead to unemployment since fewer jobs will be offered; some employers will no longer be able to afford to pay the higher wage, and more people will become part of the labor force due to the better pay. But minimum wage laws would be less necessary with the emphasis by purposive organizations on providing a living salary to their staff.

Agricultural price supports have long been criticized by economists in that they keep more farmers than are needed in the agricultural industry, create surpluses, and raise food prices. The higher food prices could then make it necessary to raise the minimum wage even more to cover the needs of workers. Food prices do fluctuate significantly because the industry is so competitive, and weather can additionally ruin a whole season's crop, making agriculture an unstable business. Many farmers allow for this, and are making a good living now; therefore, doing away with agricultural price floors, since this raises prices, still seems to be the best policy. Giving financial aid/money to farmers where natural disasters wipe out a whole season's crop could still be feasible. But agricultural producers should still leave the industry if they cannot make a living. And that would be the case with economic entities in other industries. If they can no longer consistently sell enough of, or charge enough money for, their products or services to pay living wages to the people who work there, they should close. There could be exceptions, such as for student employment.

The idea of a price ceiling is most often associated with rent control. The problem with this is that if the price is set below the market rate, shortages occur, or quality and maintenance may diminish since the landlord cannot make enough money to cover expenses. This also should be taken care of by purposive real estate enterprises that would keep rents down on the supply side, and other economic entities that would provide a living wage to their employees on the demand side. The living wage would vary by location since the rent for land varies significantly by geographic area.

The idea of advertising to increase demand beyond consumers' need for a product should go away with a switch to purposive enterprise. In such a model, simply appealing to a person's base instincts and values, as is sometimes done to increase sales, would not be done to increase profits. If sales were down, though, it would still be tempting to try to boost demand to avoid layoffs or decreases in salaries. It can hence be hoped that advertising would be limited to providing information about a product so that people become aware of its true benefits. Such advertising would be needed especially when a new product or service is introduced, or when a change in an existing good, or its price, occurs. Products would therefore be cheaper as advertising costs would go down.

4

Microeconomics

A. Maximizing Satisfaction

THE BEHAVIOR OF consumers in maximizing their own satisfaction is part of current economic theory. This idea suggests that consumers will try to equalize their marginal, or additional, satisfaction per dollar spent on the goods and services they buy. They measure satisfaction, or utility, by a hypothetical unit of measurement called the util. Utility is defined as "the want-satisfying power of a good or service."[64] Economists use an equation that illustrates this: $MUa/Pa = MUb/Pb \ldots MUz/Pz$. MU stands for marginal, or the addition to, utility and P stands for price. The a represents the first, b the second, and z is the last good purchased. While consumers do not actually sit down and make the calculation presented in the equation, they probably do try to essentially implement the equation with their purchases. The marginal, or additional, satisfaction from buying each product divided by its price is attempted to be equalized for the consumer over all products.

It has already been discussed that consumers' values can influence their buying decisions. So, they may derive utility from "buying American" or "buying organic." Such behavior does go beyond the orange-valued rational decision of obtaining the best value for your money but still can provide utility.

The theory does reiterate the position made earlier about unlimited wants being a part of a flawed current definition of economics. Utility theory postulates that at some point MU becomes negative. You can consume only so many hamburgers at one sitting before you quit eating so as to not make yourself sick. You can have only so many chairs in your living room before you start to trip over them. So again, current utility theory contradicts the current definition of economics regarding unlimited wants.

B. Labor

When talking about the branch of economics dealing with labor, economists currently treat labor objectively, or rationally, like any other good, developing graphs of the supply and demand for labor where wages are the price of labor, and workers the quantity. Of course, the fact that they even have a separate branch of the field for labor, and that a major objective of the half of the field devoted to macroeconomics is to achieve "full employment," indicates value judgments. So, here are some issues relating to values and labor. Marie Sobczak, a junior high school teacher, talked about how it was a good thing that people could now move up to a higher class by earning enough money to do so, as opposed to it previously being dependent on their family of birth. This was essentially a movement from blue values to orange that had come about with the movement from agriculture to manufacturing. With agriculture as a prevailing way of making a living, one blue value is: "Impulsivity is controlled through guilt; everybody has their proper place." Everyone had their place, class, or caste, and these usually were decided by birth. Manufacturing reflects an orange value: "Optimistic, risk-taking, and self-reliant people deserve success." So, the junior high teacher was reflecting orange values in saying birth no longer mattered regarding class, but you could now earn enough money to raise your status. But why have classes at all? This leads us to conclude that richer people are deserving of more respect than poorer people, and this is certainly a prevailing idea in our society. But there is no relationship between how much money a person makes and whether they are a moral person or not, which should be the measure of respect. One can be poor and of high, and rich and of low, character, or vice versa. And as people move to more complex values, the yellow value prevails: "The magnificence of existence is valued over material possessions."

Why should one person make more money than another? Economists talk about the distribution of income and say there are two ways of thinking about it: from the perspectives of productivity and equality. What is behind the productivity argument? Roger Miller in his textbook *Economics Today* says this: "People are rewarded according to merit, and merit is judged by one's ability to produce what is considered useful by society."[65] So, a pro athlete or CEO earns millions because they are "worth" the money. Economists have a measure for this called marginal revenue product (MRP) that talks about how much revenue is added by each additional worker. And who can argue that Michael Jordan filled seats and brought in revenue better than anyone else in professional basketball when he played? He was the highest-paid player of his time. His MRP was reflected in his salary. But was he a better player because he worked harder, or was he born with the talent to play basketball? Probably both were factors. Let us look at the worked-harder argument for income inequality. How much harder can one person work than another? Probably 120 hours per week would be the maximum time someone could work, compared with the forty-hour standard. So, this could justify salaries three times the average wage, but the discrepancy in wages is often ten to hundred times, or much more. And, of course, people working the same number of hours often have big differences in the amount of money earned. This brings us to talent. The only way to justify different salaries for different native skill levels is that God gave it to the person, and that is because he wanted that person to make the higher salary. What about God giving the talent to that person because he wanted him to use it for the betterment of mankind? Then you could argue that for people at value levels less complex than green, you have to offer the big money to get them to use their talents for God's purpose. But do you really need to offer ten to a hundred times, or more, of what others receive to entice them to use their God-given talent? Would three or five times the average salary be enough? So, with purposive economics, some possibility for advancement would be needed for those whose values are orange or less complex, but not so far as the extreme differences in wealth and income in place today.

Related to the distribution of income is risking your money. The riskier the investment, the higher the reward; and this seems reasonable. But should people be taking risks that have a 1/100,000 chance of being successful? When does it become gambling, and when does greed come into play? One could argue that many technological breakthroughs might not have been funded if big risks had not been taken. Of course, risking $100,000 when you have $10 million in the bank compared with someone who is risking their life savings involves a big difference in risk The stock market would no longer be a way to get rich quick as we go to economic organizations that earn a maximum of only 10% profit. So, this source of difference in incomes eventually would go away.

It is also argued that technology growth would be inhibited by wage limits for those with orange or lower values. This would be a major concern since technology increase is such a major factor in economic growth and has resulted in the success of capitalism. Again, the most famous idea associated with the well-known economist Milton Friedman is: "There is no such thing as a free lunch." This is an important issue in economics because Friedman attempts to bring attention to cost here. Someone has to pay for the free lunch. The government, or the taxpayer, does so with food stamps, for example. But it is possible to have a less costly lunch or better-quality goods, as countries' wealth and living standards have increased mainly due to growth in technology. This is probably the most compelling argument for huge wage differentials for inventors, but it would not justify the incredibly high salaries of CEOs, sports heroes, and popular entertainers.

Other factors to be considered in the distribution of income are jealousy and its impact on the economy. Causing jealousy is not good because people reacting in that manner are only hurting themselves. But then does the disparity in incomes hurt or help economic performance? Some could be inspired by someone's higher income to try harder to make more money themselves or possibly become discouraged because they feel they have not been treated fairly. Most people with orange values would do the former, but it is unclear if those with less-complex values would respond in a positive way. Crime could be the response of those with red, purple, and beige values, and may very well be one reason why people and gangs with those values are involved in it. But some may see crime as their only option in lower-income neighborhoods.

And again, how much should the difference between income levels be to inspire those with orange or lower values to work harder? And how much harder should someone work? Working 120, or even 60–70, hours per week may be hard on a person's health and/or family life. And they may very well be working in an occupation that is not their purpose. A doctor may be pursuing his field for income/prestige, as opposed to being a musician by passion or purpose. And many do boring repetitive assembly-line and/or dangerous jobs because of high wages, as opposed to doing what could better use their talents.

What about the yellow value "The magnificence of existence is valued over material possessions?" As more and more people progress into these values, you could have more people doing jobs they are interested in, as opposed to taking the one that makes the highest income. People with green or more complex values already tend to work in an occupation they like instead of the one that pays the highest salary. As people evolve to more complex values, a movement toward less, or even significantly reduced, income inequality, should develop.

1. Changes in Rights

Looking at values can also help explain changes in the labor market over the past 200 years. Ken Wilber has made the point that both women's liberation[66] and the abolition of slavery[67] came about because of the move to rational thought, orange values, and industrial society. He argued that it made no sense for women to be in a productive role in the blue agricultural age because using an animal-drawn plow caused a high rate of miscarriage. Since children were needed to help out on the farm, and there was a higher incidence of infant mortality, reproduction was very important. So, that is why roles were so gender-prescribed. Having women of child-bearing age behind plows made no economic sense. Wilber also said women had more political power in horticultural societies because they could use a hoe with no physical consequences, and they were quite involved in producing food in those cultures. Some factory jobs do not involve the use of upper-body strength, so women can work much more easily in them. And the information age has made it even easier for women to participate in productive role since the physical strength needed to do office jobs is usually minimal. Women's participation in the labor force has increased tremendously since 1950. It was 33.9% for females 16+ years of age in 1950 and 56.8% in 2016.[68] Also supporting this idea are studies showing that women are completing college at a higher rate than men. The four-year college completion rate at public institutions in the United States was 48.2% for women and 42.1% for men in 2016. The rates were higher for females at private four-year and two-year private and public schools as well.[69]

Retired professor Dr. Myron Ross of Western Michigan University joked in his class about how children became consumption goods, rather than capital goods, as we transitioned from the agricultural to the industrial age. But this brings attention to how important it was to have children who worked on the farm before industrialization. And once agriculture became mechanized, they were no longer needed for this. And in fact, if farmers of today have a larger family, some or most of the children need to look for work elsewhere, probably at a factory, office, or store in the city, when they grow up.

Wilber also relates this to the end of slavery. No one had said much against this institution for thousands of years until it no longer made economic sense. It was an economic argument that was made for slavery by southern US farmers who wanted to continue it at the time of the Civil War, which was before agriculture became mechanized. The north was more industrial, so slavery made no economic sense. Once agriculture became mostly mechanized, slaves for the most part were no longer useful in farming, either. Where mechanization of agriculture is still not practical, migrant workers still receive low wages.

The issue of LGBT rights, including employment rights, also is a factor in doing away with such gender-prescribed roles. If you were gay or lesbian, it did not make sense to act on it in the blue-valued agricultural age, because you would have a harder time surviving if you married someone of the same sex and could not reproduce to have help on the farm. And in the case of transgender people wanting to be a member of a different sex instead of identifying with the sex they were assigned at birth, that also made no economic sense. Males who felt more comfortable identifying as female could not reproduce, so the traditional female role did not work for them. Women preferring a male identity also faced the same issues with gendered roles: they could not impregnate a woman to obtain children to help work on the farm. But with the move to smaller families in industrialized countries, and with problems of overpopulation, reproduction is not as important as it used to be earlier and is sometimes even undesirable. So those who are LGBT are gaining more acceptance in society today. And people of this community no longer find it an economic necessity to marry someone of the opposite gender or fit into prescribed genders based solely on their biology at birth.

2. Rudolf Steiner on Labor

Rudolf Steiner wrote:

> the human labor system ought not to be controlled by the identical forces which find play in the economic life.
>
> It is by his interests, founded in the needs of the soul and spirit, that man is involved in the economic life.[70]

This lends support to the idea that people should work at what interests them the most, and not to treat labor as just another commodity. Steiner goes on to say:

> In a healthily organized society it will be manifest that labour cannot be paid for. Labour cannot have an economic price allotted to it as a set-off against a commodity. It is only the commodity produced by labour which has an economic value when set off against other commodities. The way in which a man is to work for the community, and the amount of work he is to contribute, must be regulated by considerations of his personal capacity and the conditions of a decent human existence. And for this to be so the control must originate with the political state, in complete independence of the economic administration.[71]

Steiner's idea is relevant to the current debate regarding living and minimum wage laws. His argument supports higher limits to provide a decent living for all, but stands against paying wages, which is the price of labor as a commodity. Steiner offers an alternative to wages: "And this relation will rest not on a barter of commodities (in the form of money) for labour-power, but on the apportionment of a fixed share to each of the two parties who jointly produce the commodity."[72] The two parties are the entrepreneur and the people who actually produce the commodity. Besides this different way of paying those who produce the goods and services, Steiner places great emphasis on how the entrepreneur may develop from the spiritual order, and not be influenced by either the state or the economic organization. Such development would lend support to economic entities that are concerned with the product or service being provided, and to the goal of having these organizations pay a living wage. The people coming up with the ideas would be free to put the emphasis on such a setup, and those actually producing the product or service would have a stake in it as well. There would be concern that by having no guaranteed level of income both parties would be taking the risk of not making enough to live on. But this would be a concern for anyone working for an organization today anyway. The economic organization may no longer be viable if people are unwilling to pay enough for their product. Temporary unemployment compensation could still be a solution to the concern that economic entities can fail if they do not meet society's needs. This could, as it does currently, provide income maintenance for a maximum specified time period while the employees of an organization that is no longer viable find other ways to provide income for themselves and their families. And opportunities for retraining should be provided as well and probably to a much greater extent than is currently available to workers who lose their jobs due to a lack of skills needed for the current opportunities available.

3. Labor Unions

Labor unions are controversial. Union membership as a percentage of the labor force in the United States has been declining since the 1960s.[73] A major reason is that they are the strongest in the manufacturing and government sectors. The economy has become significantly more service-oriented as opposed to goods-producing in developed countries. And so far, unions have made little progress in organizing private sector service industries, so organized labor has gone from around 20% to 11% of the workforce in the United States since manufacturing became less important. Some feel unions are no longer needed since there are more laws to protect labor, and employers themselves are more respectful of their employees than in the past. But currently, there is a countermovement aimed at providing living wages to low-wage employees. Some are trying to move pay from the minimum wage level of around $7/hour to $15/hour at fast-food restaurants. Since paying a living wage is one of the main objectives of a move to purposive economic organizations, labor unions would probably no longer be needed. But they could play a role in accelerating the process of moving to purposive enterprise by actually trying to buy out the existing owners of companies. Economic entities should be more democratic, to begin with, in an economy with 10% maximum profits. The unions would probably need to carry out such buyouts by borrowing since union dues would most likely not be sufficient to purchase a company. And purposive entities may evolve into employee-run cooperatives and would be so if the union, or employees, bought out a business.

4. Working and Child Care

One idea to explore is how families of two parents with young children not going to school a full day could work twenty hours per week at different times of the day. This would minimize child-care expenses, give families an opportunity to raise their own children, and give each parent a chance to share the joys and challenges of child-rearing. And both parents could still continue in their careers. Since many jobs are currently designed for full-time work, especially those currently paying a living wage, this plan would require a change of attitude by economic organizations. It should not hurt either parent's career that they decide to do this for five or six years. Once children are in school all day, both parents could go back to work full-time if they wish. Or if they found they preferred this way of living, they could continue working twenty hours per week and sharing child-rearing responsibilities.

C. Poverty and Income Inequality

Since economic downturns would be less likely and paying a living wage would be a principal objective of purposive organizations, poverty would be reduced, if not eliminated, as a result of the move to the new economic paradigm. And income inequality would be lower or nonexistent since workers would be less motivated by money. Currently, there is still the problem of structural unemployment. Economists define this as workers not having the skills needed to do the jobs that are available. There would need to be an improved educational system for young people and more support for retraining older workers who have lost jobs, as mentioned in the previous section.

D. Retirement and Disability

For countries with adequate retirement plans now, no change would be needed. A proposed solution in the United States would be to have employers and employees increase what they are contributing to the Social Security System now, and this money would be put into long-term bonds so interest would accrue to ensure the system is funded. Social Security benefits would also be increased to make it a living income. Many who are living only on Social Security currently have a difficult time paying for minimum needs, including food. Existing pension plans and individual savings for retirement could be done away with. This could solve the short-term problems with Social Security underfunding, and provide a comfortable living to those who retire in the future. Increased contributions to Social Security would solve the problem of people not saving enough for retirement and/or being bad at making investment decisions, or exhausting their retirement savings if a financial crisis hits a family. Changes to retirement funding would be done gradually on both the contribution and benefit side.

The whole system would be based on a disability concept. Workers would decide as to their need for partial or full retirement benefits. If people are working in jobs that is their purpose, there would be less need to retire, but as they age, they may may need to work fewer hours. If they are not working in a job that is fulfilling, they should switch jobs. Some workers may be able to contribute only so much to the productive process from an earlier age if they have some disability, similar to those who receive Social Security Disability now. This would help funding of the system, with fewer people being fully retired.

Workers would be assured of making a living income through work or the disability/retirement system, or a combination thereof. As the disability concept begins to be realized, this would very likely result in a decline in the contributions required of workers and employers as workers experience longer and probably healthier lives due to medical advances.

Relating to retirement income is the issue of workers not knowing what to do with themselves after retiring. They should truly try to figure out what they would love to do, and either supplement their income if needed, or volunteer if money is not an issue.

E. Minimizing Costs

Current economic theory has developed extensive models that account for costs on the supply side in interaction with consumer wants and needs on the demand side. On the supply side, it has come up with a theoretical long run average cost (LRAC) curve that has a U shape. The cost curve has the quantity of goods on the horizontal axis and costs on the vertical axis, as shown in Figure 4.

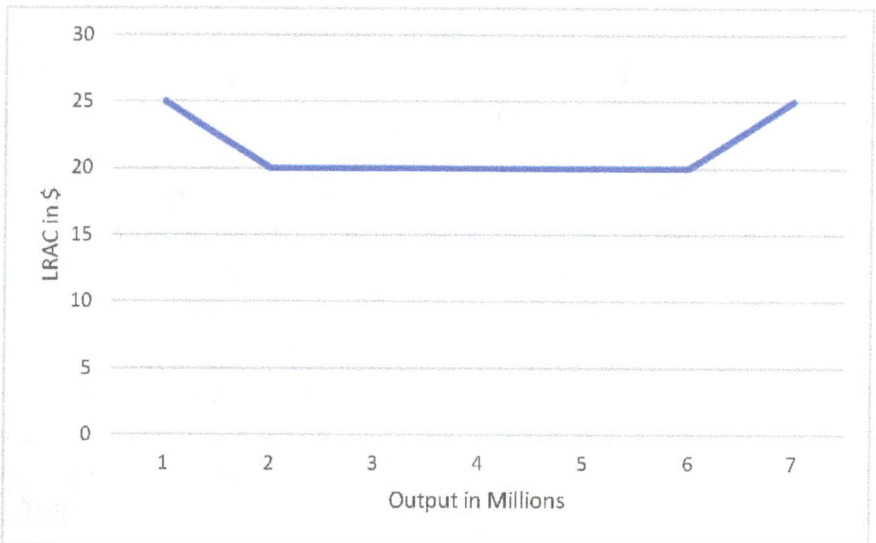

Figure 4: Long-Run Average Cost Curve.

It postulates that it is U-shaped because as larger quantities of goods are sold, companies will realize cost savings from the specialization of labor that allows employees to be more productive as they learn to be experts in their jobs. Also, more efficient machinery can be used, and possibly quantity discounts from suppliers will make inputs cheaper. So, at lower levels of output, costs decrease as the quantity is increased, and this accounts for the downward slope of the left side of the curve. It is postulated that at very high output, a large organization may become difficult to manage, and the curve starts to slope upward. This explains the U shape of the curve. Economic theory says that only if an industry is perfectly competitive will producers produce at the minimum point of the LRAC. As previously discussed, most industries are oligopolistic, and it is shown in economic models that these industries do not operate at the minimum point of the LRAC. All of this assumes that firms will be maximizing profits. See Table 2, which lists values of LRAC, marginal revenue, marginal cost, and demand. Demand shows how much people will buy at different price levels. The economic Law of Demand states that consumers will buy more as the price decreases, and less as the price increases. The marginal revenue curve tells you how much revenue is added at different output levels. The marginal cost curve shows how much is added to the cost at each quantity level. Economic theory says producers will operate at the output level where marginal revenue = marginal cost. This makes sense, for

Output (Millions)	LRAC ($)	Demand Price ($)	Marginal Revenue ($)	Marginal Cost ($)
1	15	30	30.00	15.00
2	10	25	20.00	5.00
3	10	20	10.00	10.00
4	10	15	0.00	10.00
5	10	10	−10.00	10.00
6	10	5	−20.00	10.00
7	15			45.00

Table 2: Output, LRAC, Demand Price,
Marginal Revenue, and Marginal Cost

you would try to keep producing as long as the addition to a business' revenue adds more than it does to its costs. Figure 5 shows the Table 2 values in graph form. Note that LRAC and marginal cost are equal between output levels three to six million units, so only one line shows in the graph. So, in Figure 5,

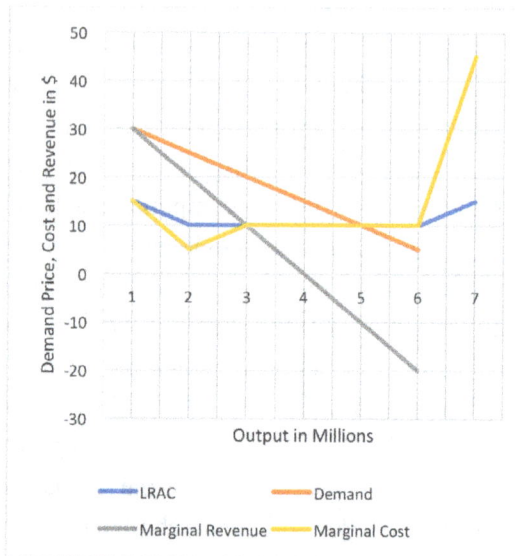

Figure 5: Profit Maximization versus Minimizing Cost

marginal revenue equals marginal cost at the three-million output and $10 level. To obtain the price you must look at the demand curve at the three-million output level, so it would be $20. This would be an excess profit of $10 per unit. This is the $20 price minus the $10 marginal cost. But if you are just covering costs, which already include a "normal" profit in economic theory, an economic organization would be operating where the demand curve for the organization's good or service intersects the LRAC.[74] That is at a price of $10 and an output level of five-million units. This is a hypothetical example, so the difference in price and output would likely not be as dramatic, but it shows what is possible. And it would depend on where the demand curve intersects the LRAC as to whether it is an item priced at the lowest cost possible. If it intersects at the downward or upward sloping portions, it would not be at the minimum level. But the intersection of the LRAC and demand curves is often striven for when regulating prices for public utilities, and that is what is advocated here. Economic organizations would voluntarily be earning a "normal" profit of at most 10%.

But costs and prices could be raised by other factors. If the enterprise was not paying its employees a living wage before it became purposive, or if it was not taking into account all costs, such as the external costs of pollution, prices could be kept at the profit maximization level or not lowered as much. Wages should be raised to a living wage level, if possible. And accountants at economic entities would now be looking to factor in the external costs that they are aware of. While this would not be an easy task, estimates can usually be made. But purposive economic entities that try to produce the best product or service they can, at the lowest price possible, should be much more likely to consider all costs, including the external ones. Since producing where the LRAC intersects the demand curve would increase the quantity produced some would be concerned that in the case of goods this could lead to more pollution. Alternatively, a living wage and covering external production costs could limit the increased output if this were a concern. Another way to limit output would be to improve the product quality, making it more costly, instead of lowering its price if producing more goods would be detrimental to the environment.

F. Competition

Competition is thought to be a key and positive component of a free market economy. It is said to keep costs down, stimulate innovation, and keep quality up as companies try to stay ahead, or at least equal, to the other firms that make the same or similar products. But sometimes producers do not compete by price but by advertising to stimulate demand. Thus, it can sometimes lead to higher costs and prices, and too much output. But purposive organizations should be limiting themselves to informational advertising so this should not be an issue.

There are antitrust laws to promote competition. These were originally passed at the end of the nineteenth century in response to firms that were driving others out of business through legal and illegal means to monopolize an industry. A monopoly exists when there is only one firm in an industry. So, if there is no competition, there is less reason to hold prices down or maintain quality. Similar to oligopolistic industries, monopolies charge higher prices and restrict quantity levels when compared with a perfectly competitive industry. The antitrust laws have been modified at various times since the late 1800s. They do not allow some company mergers if regulators think it would substantially lessen competition. For example, the regulators would usually not allow the two largest firms in an oligopolistic industry to merge. The government would also prosecute companies that meet to fix prices at a higher level than would occur if they were competing. And firms can sue each other if they can prove their rivals are not competing fairly. It is also illegal for a firm to lower its price below the market level in order to drive others out of business, and then raise it when the other companies have left the industry. Some companies are considered "natural" monopolies. One example is the electric power industry. It does not make sense to have more than one set of electric power lines running to homes, businesses, and governmental facilities. So, public utilities like electric companies and water systems are examples of "natural" monopolies. They are regulated to keep their prices down while still allowing the companies a reasonable, or "normal," profit, or else the government itself provides the service. Usually, governments run water systems. As we move further into the information age, many new services and products have arguably become natural monopolies. Examples are Microsoft's operating system, spreadsheet, and word processing software for computers, eBay, and satellite radio. While it can be argued that these companies do have some competition, in effect they are monopolies. Microsoft has been sued by governments for antitrust violations, but it does not make much sense to have more than one computer operating system because of compatibility issues and because of the time and effort needed to learn how to use a different type of software.

All the government regulations to promote competition and set prices for natural monopolies would be less necessary if economic entities were purposive ones. These entities would be charging the price where the LRAC curve intersects the demand curve.

And how would competition work over the transition period from profit-maximizing to purposive economic entities? The change would be gradual, but possibly faster than one might think. A couple of ways the first company in an industry could decide to go to normal profits have been discussed. One way it could occur is when owners with green or more complex values decide to change the business to a purposive one. Or a union, or employee group, can decide to buy out the existing owners. Since the initial company that goes purposive would probably be charging lower prices, competition would then force the other companies to follow suit. Antitrust laws may need to be changed to recognize that these organizations are not trying to drive the other companies out of business with artificially low prices, but are simply trying to provide the best product at the lowest price. They do not want to drive other organizations out of business but are in effect forcing them to be more responsible and charge lower prices that would shrink profits. But the initial purposive organization in some low-price industries would need to slowly raise wages to living levels and to account for the external costs of pollution gradually so that prices are not raised to levels above those of their competitors until the whole industry becomes purposive. The cost savings realized by reducing profits to 10% should allow higher wages and money to be spent on pollution control devices immediately if the industry is already paying a living wage. And pollution control laws equalize the playing field unless a firm has decided to limit its emissions before this is required by the rights sector. The only case where the economic sector might want to force companies to be purposive would be in the case of natural monopolies—since no or minimal competition exists in these industries, it might possibly be necessary to mandate that the industry be so. The existing natural monopolies that are regulated already are forced to charge the price where the demand curve intersects the LRAC now, and the price does include a normal profit.

Should competition continue to be subject to antitrust regulation by the governing body of the economic sector in a purposive world? These organizations should be putting their emphasis on providing the best product or service possible at an affordable cost. But it is possible that an economic entity could become complacent, or too large to be effectively managed, so it would still be good to have other producers so that innovation would be more likely.

Possibly more mergers could be allowed if a case can be made that these mergers would provide positive benefits in terms of lower costs and/or improved product quality as a result. But at the very least, no monopolies should be allowed unless they are natural ones. And Rudolf Steiner's recommendation that the organization's upper management should be replaced if it does not do the job could be applied in extreme cases. The governing body of the economic sector should be able to do this, if necessary.

Patents and copyrights are related to competition. When the government grants patents for a new invention, it allows a time period, (currently twenty years in the United States), for which the developer has an exclusive right to make, use, or sell the innovation. This is done to encourage technological change by using the profit motive. This reflects an orange value: "Progresses by learning nature's secrets and seeking out best solutions." The time limit is placed to eventually allow society full benefit from the invention while still providing producers and creative scientists an incentive to innovate and cover the costs of research and development (R&D). Certainly, in a purposive economy, the costs of R&D should be recovered by the person or organization that came up with the idea. But as values become more second-tier yellow and turquoise, the maximizing profit incentive should no longer be needed for people to realize their creative potential. The number of years patents are in effect could be gradually reduced, but not eliminated, since innovators still would need to recover costs.

5

Macroeconomics

A. Business Cycle and Gross Domestic Product

THE US ECONOMY will be used for this discussion, but the ideas here can be applied to other countries, especially the developed ones. Gross domestic product (GDP) is used by economists to measure the wealth of a nation and determine when countries are in recession or expansion. GDP is defined as "the total market value of all final goods and services produced during a year by factors of production located within a nation's borders."[75] This usually means the retail price is used, except that if a business buys a good or service in its final form, such as a machine, this is also included in GDP. Businesses are considered to buy their goods and services at the wholesale level. The prices of intermediate goods, those purchased and included in the price of the final good, such as wheat to be used by a business in making bread, are not included in GDP. These are excluded because it would be double counting to include them since the value of the wheat is already included in the final price of the bread at the retail level.

The National Bureau of Economic Research (NBER) determines the beginning and ending dates of recessions in the United States. The NBER uses GDP as a major determining measurement and has always included quarters of negative growth in the time period used for a recession. When GDP starts to increase consistently, recessions are declared to have ended.

This causes some problems since the general public thinks mainly about unemployment when thinking about recessions, and businesses often take a while to start hiring after a recession ends. They often want to be sure the recession is over before they add or recall workers. So, it takes some time after GDP starts to increase and a recession is declared officially over for unemployment to reach low-enough levels that many citizens think everyone can find a job that pays enough to pay their bills. The Great Recession is an extreme example. The NBER said it ended in the third quarter of 2009. But some of the general public in some ways did not consider it to be over even during the 2016 election. The loss of high-paying unskilled jobs to automation or outsourcing was of concern to many in the U. S. population even though the unemployment rate had been below 5% since May 2016, and this is usually considered to be the full employment level. So, while most people were employed, there were some who were not satisfied with their income level, and this was very evident among Donald Trump and Bernie Sanders supporters in the 2016 U. S. election. These candidates' promises to restrict foreign trade appealed to these voters since they thought this would bring better-paying jobs back to the United States.

Listed below are eight possible causes of a recession. They are:

1. Fiscal and monetary policy
2. The credit market
3. The stock market
4. The oil market
5. The end of a war
6. Cyclical factors
7. Trade wars
8. Pandemics

It has already been discussed how moving to purposive entities can help with the business cycle regarding the credit and stock market causes. Once every organization aims for only 10% maximum profits, there would be less incentive to speculate in the stock market. So, there would be a lower chance of large stock market swings. And if credit institutions are member-owned, there is less reason to make loans to customers that are bad credit risks for profit reasons. What about the other recession causes in this proposed new economic world?

The oil market and the ends of wars are mostly international political issues. The 1973–1975 recession was caused mainly by drastically rising oil prices resulting from the oil embargo imposed by the Organization of Petroleum Exporting Countries (OPEC). The members of OPEC were mainly Middle Eastern countries that were protesting the developed countries' support of Israel in the war in that area at the time. The 1980–1982 recession was caused by the Iranian oil embargo in the wake of the Iranian Revolution. The United States had been a big supporter of the Shah of Iran, who was overthrown at that time. So, for the most part, the oil market problems were a result of wars or revolutions. Rudolf Steiner has suggested in *The Threefold State* that the state organization he proposes would make wars less likely because of the division of states into three parts, with each negotiating as separate entities. He thought it would be harder for such a state to coordinate all three parts of a country's government, and that since all would have separate relations with other nations, it would be difficult to obtain an agreement to go to war. Regarding the drastic rises in oil prices, since 2000 this factor has not seemed to have had the drastic impact on the economy that it did before that even though there have been periods of rapid increases in oil prices. But Middle Eastern oil-exporting countries and commodities markets are volatile, so price increases are still of concern. But if oil companies were to switch to a 10% maximum profit, it would be helpful in this regard. And the consciousness and values necessary to switch to purposive organizations in developed states may make them more interested in cooperation rather than exploiting their economic or military power in other countries. So less-developed countries would have less resentment toward the developed ones for intervening in their internal affairs. And hopefully, developing countries will move toward more world-centric values that start as people move toward orange values. This may still be a problem, for orange profit-motive values can sometimes override the world-centric ones. The developed countries have demonstrated this dominance of the profit motive over world-centric values in terms of international relations, the mistreatment of labor in developing countries, and in ignoring environmental issues. And developing nations can be even worse concerning these issues.

Government fiscal and monetary policy is another cause of recessions. This usually occurs as a result of restrictive monetary policy to control inflation by a central bank, such as the Federal Reserve system in the United States. The Federal Reserve is a quasi-government institution designed to oversee the banking system that was established by the Federal Reserve Act in 1913. The employees are not US government employees, but the seven members of its board of governors, including its chair, are appointed by the president and approved by the US Senate. The members of the board of governors serve seven-year terms to try to lessen the degree to which the decisions they make are influenced by short-term politics, inasmuch as the president, senators, and House members serve four-, six-, and two-year terms, respectively. Restrictive monetary policy is designed to raise interest rates for borrowing, and it is implemented in three ways. One way is by selling US Treasury bonds. This increases the supply of bonds, forcing prices down on all bonds. If people pay less to buy a bond, this effectively raises the interest they receive on it. Assume the Federal Reserve sells a bond for $500 that is receiving $50 per year in interest. This would be 10% interest. If the bond was previously selling on the open market for $600, the bond was making only 8.3%. So, this causes other rates to rise since people now see Treasury bonds making more interest. Another way the Federal Reserve raises interest rates is by increasing the "discount rate," the rate of interest it charges banks to borrow money from them. This causes the banks to raise the interest rates they charge for loans. And a third way to influence rates is by reserve requirements for money they hold on deposit at the Federal Reserve. Banks are less likely to loan money if they have to hold a higher percentage of money at the Federal Reserve, and lowering reserve requirements makes more money available to lend.

So, when interest rates rise, businesses and consumers are less likely to buy goods and services if it is more expensive to borrow. If less is purchased, GDP declines. If less is bought, businesses start charging less for their products or services, and inflation goes down. Prices are closely watched by the Federal Reserve because if they go up too fast, the result is instability in the economy, and stagflation can occur.

Stagflation is when GDP decreases, causing unemployment, and prices go up at the same time. Usually, inflation and unemployment go in opposite directions. If the GDP increases, there is a tendency for businesses to hire more people and also raise prices since the demand for goods and services increases. And the opposite occurs if the GDP goes down. But if prices rise too rapidly, the uncertainty can cause consumers to buy less, and businesses to invest less, causing GDP to decline. That is stagflation.

Some recessions have occurred because the effort to control inflation through interest rate increases went too far—the higher rates reduced consumer and business spending too much, and GDP went into the negative growth range.

But if businesses are not focused on maximizing profits, inflation should be less of a problem. Economists currently worry more about deflation than inflation. This is because if prices start falling, profits go down, and wages may also go down as a result. But if economic entities are focused on minimizing prices while providing a living wage to their employees, deflation should not be a problem. It would be desirable, in fact, because it would effectively cause a continual increase in living standards since economic entities would be continually reducing costs due to innovation. But what about an improved, or new, product or service that would be more expensive to provide? Supply and demand would solve this issue. As an extreme example, a million-dollar car would simply be unaffordable for almost everyone as incomes become more equal, so none would be produced.

Restrictive government fiscal policy is much less cited as a cause of recessions. This occurs when the government deliberately increases taxes and/or cuts spending to slow down inflation. If taxes are increased, people have less money to buy goods, thus decreasing GDP. If the government cuts spending, it reduces GDP since government purchases are included. Politicians almost never do either of these things since neither policy helps them to be popular with the voters. It is rare that elected representatives support higher taxes unless they are serving their last terms and do not need to worry about reelection. And while cutting government spending is more popular with the voters, if it costs jobs in a politician's particular geographic community, or it is a program his or her constituents use, a politician will rarely vote to eliminate it. Politicians usually let the Federal Reserve use restrictive monetary policy to control inflation. As discussed earlier, this would be much less needed as we move toward purposive economic organizations.

So, if other causes of inflation and recession reduce the problems of the business cycle, there simply would be less need to use restrictive or expansionary fiscal and monetary policies in the economy. And it would be less likely these tools would be overused and cause the problems they are supposed to eliminate.

Recessions are also blamed on cyclical factors, with the idea that the economy naturally goes into recession every so often. This is not much discussed in economics today. Some economists have tried to come up with mathematical models to explain these cycles without much success. But the stock and credit markets do seem prone to periodic meltdowns, as has been argued previously in this book. If there is lessened stock market speculation, and credit institutions are nonprofit member-owned organizations, this would seem to help moderate, or end, any possible "natural" cycle in these markets and the economy overall.

Another cause of recessions is trade wars. These have been cited as making the Great Depression worse. Most economists think that free trade is a better way to go. When higher tariffs, which are taxes on foreign goods, are instituted, those taxes make those goods more expensive. So, tariffs could mean more sales and jobs for domestic producers. But the producers of that product in the country instituting the tariffs either provide an inferior product or charge higher prices, than their foreign competitors. Otherwise, the domestic country's consumers and businesses would not be buying foreign products. So, for example, President Trump put tariffs on steel. This may help the domestic producers and add jobs in that industry in this country but may hurt the businesses that buy steel since they will need to raise their prices to account for the higher cost. This will reduce sales and possibly lead to layoffs in industries that buy steel. And an additional problem may arise if the country or countries having to pay the tariffs on steel start putting them on US products they are buying. So, if foreign countries tax, for example, bread, in retaliation for the steel tariff, then US bakeries would lose sales and possibly jobs. This may actually hurt the GDP of all countries involved in the trade wars if more jobs are lost than gained, and possibly lead to a recession. Since purposive enterprises would be paying living wages, there would be less reason for workers to call for trade barriers and less of a possibility for a recession to be caused by a trade war. But if jobs were being lost due to free trade, a recession would still be a possibility. More will be said about free trade in the section devoted to that topic.

The pandemic that began in the year 2020 made it obvious that a recession can result when this health crisis occurs. Purposive economic organizations might reduce layoffs if the amount of money saved by the entity were adequate. Alternative responses to reduced operations, such as temporarily lowering salaries instead of reducing the number of employees on their payroll might be more common than in businesses that maximize profits.

Moving to purposive economic entities and Steiner's Threefold State should lessen or even eliminate the business cycle. The stock market would be less volatile, and the credit market would be less likely to make bad loans. Oil producers that had a 10% maximum profit should make this market more stable. Fewer wars due to the Threefold State would lessen this factor in the business cycle. And oil inflation does not seem to have the impact on the business cycle it used to. Deflation is more likely, and desirable, with purposive organizations, so restrictive monetary and fiscal policy would be less likely to be used. Therefore, the danger of recession resulting from deflation would also diminish. And the call for trade wars could lessen as economic enterprises work toward paying a living wage. Possibly purposive enterprises could come up with layoff alternatives in the case of pandemics. So, the business cycle itself could be moderated, or eliminated, in a purposive world.

B. Money

Economists talk about four functions of money. They are listed below with a definition:

1. "Medium of Exchange—Any item sellers will accept as payment"[76]
2. "Unit of Accounting—A measure by which prices are expressed, the common denominator of the price system"[77]

3. "Store of Value—The ability to hold value over time"[78]
4. "Standard of Deferred Payment—A property of an item that makes it desirable for use as a means of settling debts maturing in the future"[79]

So, money is a practical medium that makes economic transactions more efficient than a barter system. It is much easier to exchange money than to try to trade so many chickens for so many toasters. But money also relates to people's values. As discussed in the section on labor, money is used as a measure of status by people with orange or less-complex values. The result is that people who have high MRPs, such as sports stars and CEOs, desire salaries way beyond their needs, while there is a lack of self-worth among those with low incomes. And if one is unemployed, it means a person must live on a reduced income and/or savings. Lack of a job raises people's anxiety levels also, in most cases, for fear that they will not have enough money to pay their bills. The first six valueMEMES are "subsistence" memes, so money has a lot more significance than just its functions. Status and anxiety issues come into play. As we move to a society in which more people with green and more complex values are less concerned with social standing, and purposive economic entities result in less unemployment, lessening the fear of scarcity, money could be used more in its functional role in the future.

A world currency could solve some problems. Poorer countries would have a stable currency. Speculation in currency trading would be eliminated, contributing to stabilization, and countries would not be able to manipulate their currency to gain trade advantages. Countries like Japan and China have kept their currency artificially devalued to make their exported products cheaper. A disadvantage of having a world currency would be that it would be difficult to use monetary policy at the national level since it would need to be implemented worldwide. But there would be less need to do so if economies are more stable.

Possibly alternative money systems like Bitcoin, or using credits on cellphones as is being done in Kenya, might move us toward this without using the United Nations. Bitcoin has not been stable, so this may not be the answer, but technology may come up with a solution.

C. National Debt

What about national debts? They increase when the government borrows money to fund spending in excess of taxes and revenues collected. Government spending and taxes should decline in a Threefold State with a 10% maximum profit economic sector for four major reasons: less spending on welfare and unemployment benefits, national defense, police protection, and government retirement programs.

If the business cycle is smoothed out, with less unemployment, as a result of transitioning to purposive economic entities, this would reduce money spent on welfare and unemployment income-maintenance programs. Welfare spending should be reduced due to there being more jobs available with a smoothed-out, or nonexistent, business cycle. Since economic organizations could still go out of business as their products or services are no longer needed in the economy, the unemployment benefits program would still be needed to help people transition to new work, and possibly for those with seasonal jobs. And it would lower employer costs for unemployment insurance since their rates are based on their rate of layoffs. If a Threefold State did reduce wars as Rudolf Steiner suggests, less would be spent on defense. And if people moved to working at jobs that reflect their purpose; they would be less likely to retire until they physically and/or mentally could no longer perform their job. This would reduce the use of retirement programs like Social Security.

Taxes would be reduced once existing national debts were paid off since government budgets would be smaller. Since the move to purposive economic entities would be a gradual one, this would not solve existing national debt problems in the near term.

The new economy would hopefully lead to a smaller or nonexistent government debt.

D. Taxation System

What type of taxation system would there be under this new economic paradigm? As has already been discussed, there would be less corporate income tax revenue, and probably lower taxes, in general. Economics currently talks

about two theories of taxation: the benefits-received and ability-to-pay principles. The benefits-received theory says that those who receive services should
pay for them. This would be a justification for taxes on gasoline going to pay
for road construction and maintenance. The ability-to-pay principle says that
those who have more income should pay a higher proportion of it than those
who make less money. The principle here is that the higher your income, the
more ability you have to pay taxes now. Someone with low income who can
barely pay, or not cover, their bills would have less ability to afford taxes, so
they should pay a smaller or even zero or negative proportion of taxes on their
income. The higher someone's income, the more likely they would be able to
spare the money, so the higher the income is, the greater the proportion that
they could afford to pay in taxes. This is the justification for a progressive tax
system where the greater your income is, the greater the percentage of income
paid in taxes. The current income tax system used by the United States and
many developed countries is progressive. An alternative proposal advanced by
some is a tax where everyone pays the same proportion of their income. This
seems fairer to some since higher incomes would still pay more money, but the
percentage would be the same. But it would involve a major shift in taxes from
the higher- to middle- and low-income residents if the existing government
services were to continue without borrowing. Since incomes should be more
equal as more and more economic entities become purposive, a proportional
tax would be more likely to be implemented.

The United States uses corporate and personal income taxes for a majority
of its revenues. The major taxes used by local and state governments in the
United States are income, sales, and property taxes. It is argued that the sales
tax is regressive since the lower someone's income, the higher the proportion
of it that they are likely to spend on goods and services. Again, with more
equal incomes, the sales tax would be less regressive, but it would still be
regressive, so a move to replace it with income taxes would seem to be fairer.

Property taxes were the major tax when the United States began, and
this made sense from an ability-to-pay perspective since a large proportion
of the population was engaged in farming. But since a very small portion of
the population farms now, this tax falls on homeowners, and some portion of
apartment rental is passed on to the consumer, so this seems to be a tax on

the basic need of shelter. The State of Michigan lowered property taxes in the 1990s and replaced them with an increase in sales tax. This was popular, but the higher sales tax is regressive although somewhat tempered since Michigan does not tax food bought from grocery stores. This avoids taxing a basic need. An increase in the income tax would have been better, but it is a proportional tax in that state.

"The unearned increment from land"[80] is a concept used by economist John Stuart Mill in his book *Principles of Political Economy*. It relates to increases in land values that accrue to landowners as a result of no effort on their part. This can occur as land nearby is more intensely developed as an area becomes more popular for agriculture, residential, or commercial development. Henry George made the case that this unearned increment should be taxed, and possibly it could be the only tax:

> But when, as we propose, economic rent, the "unearned increment of wealth," is taken by the state for the use of the community, then land will pass into the hands of users and remain there, since no matter how great its value, its possession will be profitable only to the users and remain there.[81]

Land speculation to realize profits from this unearned increment was a contributor to the housing/financial crisis that led to the Great Recession. So, a tax on the "unearned increment" when real estate is sold would stop this type of speculation, and provide further stability for the economy. One principle of the new economy regarding earning income in a field where your true contribution to mankind can be realized could be reinforced with a tax on land sales gains. But since many people own their own homes, and one reason they do purchase them is to realize this gain, this would not be a popular tax. There was a tax on the income from this when property was sold in the United States, but this was done away with except for more expensive homes. The gain could be taxed at 100% for economic entities, and for increases in value over the average price of a home for individuals and families in an area, at least. The property tax can be justified somewhat under the benefits-received principle since the more valuable the land, the more one has to lose from fire, vandalism, home robbery, and being conquered by a foreign power. On the other hand, police protection and national defense are often cited by economists as difficult to assess in terms of how much benefit an individual receives from these government services if one is never attacked, or does not lose someone close to them in a war, or similarly never needs police protection. How much does police and military presence protect someone who does not personally experience these events? It would be difficult to know how much the presence of police and military personnel protects someone's home.

Henry George also wanted to tax any unearned gain from the actual rental of property. He actually wanted no ownership of land, so it would be valuable only to those who use it. This would stop landlords from increasing rent as real estate values increase in an area. If no one owns any land, disputes over who could use it would occur. And a 100% tax on rental income would mean no one would rent out property. But as the rental industry moves to purposive enterprise, the problem of increasing rents for non-cost-related reasons would go away. Some cost-related reasons could be maintenance, inflation, or property tax increases.

Gains from the appreciation of stock values could be considered similar to those for land. It is an unearned increment. But if we taxed all the gains, no one would buy stock, and this would go against the principle of gradually and voluntarily moving to 10% maximum profit economic entities. It is also argued that such gains are a reward for taking a risk since the person investing in a company is not guaranteed a gain and could realize a loss. Still, taxing stock gains at a higher rate could be advocated. But they are currently being taxed at a lower rate than other income because it is maintained that the person is taxed twice on it. Profits and dividends are lower due to the corporate income tax making stock gains less, and then stock gains and dividends are taxed again with the personal income tax. But taxing capital gains at a higher rate, or at least the same rate, as other income might be a good idea. This could be advocated based on such gains being an unearned increment in income.

But overall, in the purposive economic society proposed here, it would seem that a proportional income tax would be best for all levels of government. Higher, but more equal, earners would still pay more of their income, but hopefully, all would be making at least a living wage. And remember, overall taxes should be lower since there would be less need for government regulation, national defense, and police protection for theft purposes at least. A justification can also be made for a 100% tax on the "unearned increment" from the increase in land values, but for individuals and families, this should be only on gains over the average value of homes in the area. This would include the sale of real estate by economic entities since they could also realize gains from real estate sales due to no effort on their organization's part. And property taxes on economic organizations could be justified by the benefits-received principle for police and fire protection and national defense.

E. Economic History and Growth

The history of economics is studied by economists, but generally, they cover only from roughly 1700 until now, and pretty much only the period beginning with the Industrial Revolution. Earlier economic history has been largely ignored by economists. But by putting more emphasis on values and their relation to the major modes of production of Wilber's Major Epochs (Social), technological economic history becomes more important. Economics actually started with the organized hunt, which was used by hominids, the evolutionary predecessors of *Homo sapiens*. Jürgen Habermas wrote:

> If we examine the concept of social labor [economy] in the light of more recent anthropological findings, it becomes evident that it cuts too deeply into the evolutionary scale; not only humans but hominids too were distinguished from the anthropoid apes in that they converted to reproduction through social labor and developed an economy. The [hominid] adult males formed hunting bands, which (a) made use of weapons and tools (technology), (b) cooperated through a division of labor, and (c) distributed the prey within the collective (rules of distribution). The making of the means of production and the social organization of labor, as well as the distribution of its products, fulfilled the conditions of an economic means of reproducing life.[82]

As already noted, mankind progressed from the organized hunt to horticulture, then agriculture, and further developed with industrialization. We are now in the information age, and this has affected economics, and probably will change this science quite a bit if purposive enterprise comes to fruition.

The increase in GDP divided by a country's population, or per capita GDP, is currently used by economists as the measure of economic growth. Since the Industrial Revolution, GDP has increased over time in many countries, except during recessions, indicating that its citizens have become wealthier. This has resulted in the middle class becoming the largest segment of the population in developed countries.

Spiral Dynamics is very relevant to economic development. Economists have already emphasized the importance of human capital (education and training) for economic development. Education usually emphasizes rational thought, and this emphasis corresponds to industrial production. But even though many in a culture can think rationally, if the values are blue or red, that can hinder economic development. Eventually, though, the ability to adopt more perspectives through rationality could make people question the traditional values that make economic progress difficult in less-developed countries, or inner cities of more advanced economies. This general growth in rationality reinforces the current emphasis by economists on human capital, or education and training, as being important for economic development.

The manufacturing jobs are growing in developing countries of Asia as orange values begin to dominate over the old, blue agricultural ones. Value-MEMES can shed a lot of light on economic development. This helps explain how China and India finally have been able to experience economic growth, and why US population groups in inner cities and less-developed countries with red and blue values have failed to make progress. While the problem of racism in connection with US states' inner cities should not be discounted, members of gangs have red values, and members of churches often have blue traditional values. Improving educational institutions that develop rational thinking in inner cities can help the movement toward the orange values needed for economic development. China, India, and other Far East Asian nations had enough people thinking rationally because of education to start moving these countries forward. If orange values and rational thinking can be instilled in the young of other less-developed areas to the 10% level that Ken Wilber thinks is necessary to make a difference in moving a culture forward, economic development is more likely.

But as developed countries move to a purposive economy, it is possible that economic development as measured by GDP per capita may become less important. As more people embrace the yellow value of "The magnificence of existence is valued over material possessions," and fewer are concerned with economic insecurity and status conveyed by money, there may be more emphasis on evolution itself as mankind continues to progress. This should also help with environmental concerns as fewer resources should be used up. But for now, the GDP per capita increase is important for less-developed countries and inner cities to help eliminate poverty, and GDP growth is needed to ensure economic stability.

Chapter 6 will give an example of using Ken Wilber's integral theories for use in sustainable economic development. The chapter will also discuss how cultures with different values progress from one valueMEME to the next, so the idea of moving to 10% maximum profit economic entities would not necessarily be the best move for economic development in a country where much of the population has blue or less-complex values. They may need to embrace orange values and capitalism and industrialization first. The importance of taking into consideration a culture's stage when examining economic development will be expanded upon in Chapter 6.

F. Free Trade

Currently, free trade is advocated by most economists. Free trade means not using quotas and tariffs (taxes on imported goods) to protect domestic industries from foreign producers, who have better or lower-priced products or services. The theory of comparative advantage is used to support the free-trader position. Economists use a simple model of two countries specializing in what they are best at producing, even if one of them is more efficient at making both goods. If each country specializes in producing what it is relatively better at doing, more goods are made. Table 3 shows this.

Before Specialization	Grain Production	Fruit Production
Country A	20	60
Country B	10	30
Total	30	90
After Specialization	Grain Production	Fruit Production
Country A	0	100
Country B	40	0
Total	40	100

Table 3: Increased Production Due to Specialization.

Table 3 shows that ten more units of grain (40–30=10) and fruit (100–90=10) are produced after each country specializes in growing what it is comparatively good at. Some economists counter this argument with the infant industry argument. This says that a country should be allowed to protect a new industry with taxes and quotas until the country is able to reach a level where it can compete with more experienced producers. The United States did this in the 1800s until it could compete with European countries; and Asian countries, such as Japan, China, and South Korea, also showed success in economic development as they protected new industries with tariffs. One factor, previously stated in the section on economic history and growth, is that Asian countries have been successful because they had enough people at the rational level of consciousness with corresponding orange values. But another factor that supports the infant industry argument is that when a less-developed country specializes in its comparative advantage, it may then be relegated to agricultural production whether the country has enough people with orange values and corresponding cognition levels or not. If it does, then comparative advantage could keep a country from industrializing and adopting the technology associated with that developmental level. And if the agricultural sector has been industrialized with mechanized labor-saving equipment, it would require fewer workers on the land with no industrial replacement jobs for them to go to.

This would lend credibility not only to the idea of using the infant industry protectionism until a country can compete but also to the idea of using free trade within a country and between developed countries. China became a powerful economy after it adopted free markets within its borders as it developed but restricted competition with foreign countries. But the free trade of the developed nations of the European Common Market has been successful. Brexit and the election of Donald Trump, and his renegotiation of the North American Free Trade Agreement (NAFTA) and other trade deals, have challenged this idea. But the University of Michigan has done a study showing that jobs could be lost in the United States by withdrawing from NAFTA. It estimated that Michigan would gain 6,400 jobs if Canada and Mexico did not institute retaliatory tariffs. But if they did, Michigan would lose 7,000 jobs, and the whole country would see employment decline by 300,000.[83] A new agreement was reached between the three countries, which is somewhat more restrictive than the previous one, but hopefully, it will not have much negative impact on jobs.

Another form of protectionism, or a way to restrict free trade, is the devaluing of a country's currency to make its products cheaper in foreign markets, and exports to that country more expensive. Countries should stop manipulating their currencies to make their exported goods cheaper and those imported into their country more expensive. An example of how this works can be seen if we consider what happens when the Canadian dollar goes from being equal to the US dollar to only being worth 90% of it. Someone with US currency can now pay only $0.90 to buy products or services from Canada. Conversely, it will now take about $1.11 for a Canadian to buy something made in the United States. As a result, people and businesses in the United States buy more Canadian goods, and Canadians buy fewer US products. This is the advantage of deliberately devaluing your currency, and it is a form of protectionism. Currencies can be devalued in different ways such as through inflation, lowering interest rates, or simply declaring your currency is worth less. Japan and China have been accused of doing this. It is not okay for a developed country like Japan to do this, but it might be more acceptable in China as a form of the infant industry argument until the country is no longer considered less developed.

Overall, free trade would be considered the goal in the long run. And it is the category of more world-centric and egalitarian traits that becomes more valued as values become more complex. World-centric values start at the orange level of complexity. People with blue or less-complex values are more focused on what is best for their country, or possibly even a more local-ized geographic area within a country in the cases of those with red, purple, or beige values. The information age makes the world a global village, and respecting the values of all people/cultures is especially strong, starting with the green value of "Spreads the earth's resources and opportunities equally among all," as shown in Table 1.

G. Outsourcing

Closely related to free trade is outsourcing. This occurs when a domestic com-pany employs foreign labor to help produce its product or service. Outsourcing is controversial, especially if there is less than full employment in, or work is shifted out of, the home country of the company doing the outsourcing. Again, those with values less complex than orange would be the most likely people to make an argument against outsourcing. Free market economics advocates, especially those with orange values, see this as the company doing what it is supposed to do to maximize profits if the work can be done more cheaply, or more efficiently, elsewhere. They also argue that domestic consumers benefit from lower prices and/or better-quality products as a result of outsourcing. Those with more complex values, especially green, may present counter-argu-ments that foreign labor is being exploited with poverty-level wages, and/or the foreign country has less stringent environmental laws. A green value in Table 1 is "Spreads the earth's resources and opportunities equally among all." Pollution squanders the earth's resources, and equal wages may not be paid in the foreign country. Those in the yellow and turquoise valueMEMES would see that there is truth in all these arguments, and search for a more harmonious solution to the question of outsourcing. This relates to the Table 1 yellow value: "Differences can be integrated into interdependent, natural flows." Moving to 10% maximum profit economic entities may be a way to make free trade and outsourcing less controversial if smaller boom-and-bust business cycles result in less unemployment and more equal wages worldwide. Those with blue and less-complex values are less likely to be arguing against free trade and outsourcing if the economy is at full employment paying a living wage, such as during the boom time of the late 1990s in the United States, but if there is an economic downturn, these issues become more controversial. Fewer people in the United States were complaining about NAFTA, a free trade agreement between Canada, the United States, and Mexico, during the economic prosperity of the end of the twentieth century than they are during the aftermath of the Great Recession.

6

Environmental Economics
and Economic Growth

ENVIRONMENTAL ECONOMICS IS usually considered a microeconomics topic, but since the sustainability study that will be cited in this section also deals with the macroeconomic topic of economic growth, this section will be dealt with separately.

The major ideas of environmental economics currently are these: considering external costs as well as private costs of economic entities, equating the marginal benefit to the marginal cost of environmental regulation, and emissions trading.

The private cost of firms is simply the cost involved in producing the product they sell. This would include rent, machinery, salary, and input costs. The external costs would be any pollution costs that would negatively impact other people and the environment. Adding external costs to the private costs constitutes what economists call the social cost. The current economic solutions to the environmental problem involve regulation. The government would tax polluters or simply restrict the levels of how much contaminants they are allowed to discharge into the environment. For example, economists advocate that the government equates the marginal, or additional, cost to the marginal benefit regarding the percentage of clean air to decide what an acceptable level of a particular pollutant is. The economic organization would then be regulated by taxation to discourage pollution and help pay for cleanup, or simply be given a standard for how much is an acceptable level of pollution. Emissions trading involves giving companies permits for how much pollution they are allowed, and if one firm is doing less than its quota, it can then sell its permits to another company that finds it cheaper than to install pollution control equipment. The desired level of pollution is achieved, and the economic entity buying the permits will probably realize greater profits and higher salaries, and charge lower prices, since its costs are not increased as much. This would not change much in a purposive economic world since it would be easier for the rights sector of a state, or international organizations, to assess how much air and water pollution is acceptable for any geographic area rather than having each individual firm trying to do so. It would be the rights sector that would decide this as having no health or environmental issues resulting from the discharge of chemicals and gases into air and water would be seen as a right. But the economic entity itself would also voluntarily try to consider its external costs as one of the goals of moving to be a purposive enterprise.

But environmental economics involves only a couple of the numerous ways to look at ecology. The book *Integral Ecology* by Michael Zimmerman and Sean Esbjorn-Hargens identifies over 200 perspectives, or schools of thought, that are available to look at ecology issues.[84] Ideally, all would be considered when looking at the issue of the environment. But practically, it would be best to take as many as possible into account when confronting an environmental issue. At the very least, all the human (some schools of ecology try to look at perspectives of the animals themselves as much as is humanly possible) groups affected by an issue should be involved in making decisions about an ecological problem. This is shown in the case studies listed in *Integral Ecology*. One of these studies will be summarized below. This is especially relevant to environmental economics since it involves economic development.

The case study is titled *Integrating Interiority in Sustainable Community Development: A Case Study with the San Juan del Gozo Community, El Salvador*. Gail Hochachka of the Drishti: Centre for Integral Action, Vancouver,

Canada, is the author and director of the study. It was conducted for nine months, from 2000 to 2002. She writes:

> Including "interiority" in development is unique to conventional and alternative development practices, and this analysis suggests it is necessary for sustainability. In other words, while the planet is surely in need of sustainable ways of living, sustainability is not arrived at merely by systemic interventions; rather it also requires a deeper understanding of, and engagement with, interpersonal and personal dimensions such as worldviews, values, and motivations. Integral community development works in three domains of Practical (action/application), Interpersonal (dialogue/process), and Personal (self-growth/reflection), and engages the developmental nature of worldviews. Using this approach in a case study in El Salvador, research outcomes showed increased collaboration and self-reflection, where economic objectives merged with equity and environmental concerns.[85]

Note that talk of values and development would relate to Spiral Dynamics valueMEMES. And the discussion of the interior and the Practical (Exterior Reality), Interpersonal, and Personal relate to the quadrants and the True, the Good, and the Beautiful, respectively, that were talked about at the beginning of this book.

El Salvador is a country that illustrates a continuing problem with economic development in less-developed countries. Much of any increase in GDP goes to the wealthiest, with little effect in helping much of the population out of poverty, and Hochachka says this is due to forgetting the interior dimensions of reality and can be responsible for environmental problems as well:

> This partiality in the focus on development on primarily economic and material indicators results in asymmetrical development. Attention and investment from development interventions goes toward building hard capacity, technology, infrastructure, and the techno-economic base, yet less focus and resources are directed toward

developing the soft capacity of the society, cultural well-being, social capital, and the psycho-cultural base for the country. This asymmetry in development's focus may be one of the key barriers for sustainability as well, as we will soon explore. This elucidates the central questions of this case study, namely what is development, and how can development expand its focus to integrate more of reality in its definition and process, particularly to include communities, ecosystems, and interiority.[86]

Hochachka also says that failed efforts in development can be attributed to ignoring interior realities:

> Repeatedly, across the planet, we see the vestigial remains of these isolated interventions: a latrine to support access to clean water is misunderstood and stands unused; a fancy building built as offices for highly trained workers remains empty; a policy envisioned by one politician is overridden by the subsequent politician and the deforestation continues. These interventions are not inherently wrong, but they are partial, and that partiality does not give rise to long-term sustainable results. My research has found that when the thinking behind development shifts to integrate exterior and interior dimensions of social change, the methodologies and approaches used also shift, including more of reality in the development process, and often the results actually begin to stick.[87]

It actually was found that the personal development (upper-left quadrant) of the people involved in a sustainable economic project helped with its success:

> This research also found that when practitioners themselves are engaged in personal growth (i.e., with conscious practices that support their own personal development), their ability to work toward an Integral community development increases. It is through their own personal growth that practitioners are more able to consistently access expansive, less self-contracted awareness (i.e., less anthro-

pocentric and egocentric) and are able to let go of personal and/or professional agendas. This seems to manifest as humility, a willingness to not know all the answers, and to meaningfully work with the community in addressing local concerns.[88]

The problems associated with including interior dimensions are discussed:

> Without the right ways to engage in subjectivity, it can be a simply bewildering domain of human life—how does one deal with beliefs, faith, values conflicts, and psychopathologies, especially if one's training has been in a single scientific field?[89]

And Hochachka writes that "subjectivity is so 'messy' compared with the 'cleanliness' of science. Understandably, yet unfortunately, the field of conventional development tends to just leave this subjective dimension out, perhaps even merely for lack of means to work with it."[90]

Examples are given in the study of the problems that can occur when interiority is ignored. This is one of them:

> A final example of this can be seen with forest conservation efforts that focus primarily on the interlocking social, economic, political, and ecological systems of the issues. This approach may initially seem quite successful. However, without "the interior buy-in" (such as alignment with values, motivation, cultural resonance) from community people, from the larger society, and from the consumers, often the gains made for systems change is quickly rolled back.

> This modern, conventional approach (what would be called "orange altitude" in Integral Theory terms) emphasizes the "expert" with his or her interventions and engaged in a one-way relationship that treats local people more as objects than subjects in their own futures.[91]

Hochachka says some people with green values working in development have started to address interiors, but have avoided the issue of hierarchy:

> These horizontal relationships between subject and subject in a co-creative process brought their own important and notable advances. The horizontality that is important for such a relationship was applied across the board in an attempt to address and rectify the persistent inequities in society. Addressing power issues is definitely achingly important, yet by reducing all hierarchies for fear of *power* hierarchies, the interior natural holarchies (nested whole-parts) of self-development were left out of consideration.

> Today, while such terms like "personal growth" and "self-empowerment" are often used in a postmodern discourse (especially in the fields of sustainability and international development), surprisingly few practitioners ask the question "How do people grow?" Interestingly, that question cannot be answered without acknowledging a holarchy of being and becoming—which is something that the alternative approach is hesitant to accept for fear of opening the door to dominating hierarchies.[92]

Hochachka talks about how an Integral Ecology approach is the answer to both the issues of using interiors and growth, but not dominator hierarchies, in development:

> The Integral Ecology approach expands and deepens the practice of sustainable community development, providing a rigorous framework for including both the dimensions of context, culture, and consciousness as well as methodologies we will need to employ to do so. It balances the emphasis on transferring technology or boosting economic growth, to also include the dialogical connection to culture and context, and to also acknowledge and work with the nuanced holarchy of personal and cultural transformation. Without

these latter arenas of practice, community development efforts are bound to partiality. And partial solutions simply cannot address very complex challenges.[93]

The Integral Ecology approach to development is summarized as:

> At the same time, rough estimates suggest a large percentage of the population has a world-view at sociocentric or lower.[94] Considering even this estimate, since most of the environmental and/or development messages used in communities today actually come from a world-centric perspective of the problems at hand, these messages are not necessarily connecting with where the majority of people are coming from. In other words, the world-centric communication is often over the heads of community people, which is not only disrespectful but ultimately ineffective.

> Thus, in this case study, I am suggesting two key points regarding the developmental nature of worldviews for sustainable development. First, sustainable development lies not only in new, ecologically sound institutions, management, and laws, but also in our collective and individual growth toward and beyond world-centrism. At the same time, practitioners need to be able to work better with where individuals and communities are actually coming from: using skillful means in communicating to different worldviews so that community people can hear and resonate, and/or creating conditions for healthy translations at the stages of consciousness that are present.[95]

A worldview beyond world-centric that corresponds to yellow and turquoise values is

> such that while one is even more compassionately called to action, there is a simultaneous letting go of the gravity of outcomes. This

Kosmocentric view reflects another core component of Integral Ecology: while the state of the environment is likely getting worse, aspects of this change are getting better, and simultaneously it is all simply perfect.[96]

The term "perfect" relates to an enlightened view of reality in which everything is seen as okay from a larger spiritual view even though it is not so in the manifest world.

Using Ken Wilber's Integral Model

The study used Ken Wilber's Integral Model of reality as a guide to design the project. It was stated by Hochachka that at a minimum, the four quadrants and levels of development should be used. Other aspects of Wilber's model that can be used are multiple lines of development, types, and states of consciousness. Evolutionary economics as used in this book uses the values, cognitive, and needs lines of development and their associated technologies. Wilber identifies around twenty other lines of development, such as emotional, kinesthetic, moral, and musical. Masculine and feminine typologies can be used, as well as personality types such as the Enneagram and Myers–Briggs classifications. And states of consciousness such as waking, dreaming, and dreamless sleep, and corresponding meditative states where a person can achieve dreaming, and dreamless sleep levels of consciousness, while awake are also considered.

Hochachka details how the Integral Model can be used in theory for economic development, using the quadrants and levels. She talks about the right-hand objective exterior quadrants as the Practical. The lower-left interior collective quadrant is called the Interpersonal, and the upper-left interior individual is referred to as the Personal.

She writes, "The Practical domain of *action/application* includes fulfilling ecological, economic, social, and political needs through various types of 3rd-person perspective interventions, such as infrastructures, management plans, institutional designs, and technical capacities."[97] The Interpersonal involves interactions with both members of the community being developed that would be impacted and with colleagues that would be involved. Hochachka also writes about members of the area being developed, saying that:

> By including dialogue in development, local people become active subjects in, rather than passive objects of, the development process. This "We" space in community development not only fosters political empowerment but also creates space to explore concerns, ideas, and goals with each other, and to really hear each other's situations, values, and stories.[98]

The Personal "enables individuals to better understand their current and potential role in effecting positive change in their community, as well as their individual impact on each other and the environment."[99]

She discusses translation and transformation regarding levels of development. Translation involves healthily living at the level of consciousness where a person is situated. This would also involve "translating key communications (about sustainability, for example) into the local worldviews of community people."[100] She talks about transformation:

> Development practitioners in Sri Lanka say that through meditative practice, individuals are motivated and mobilized to act for the development of the village, with a more connected and compassionate perspective; "only through inner transformation can the outside world change." Finally, developmental psychology research has found that transformation tends to occur in some of the following circumstances: (1) when life conditions (in all quadrants) enable growth to a subsequent stage, (2) when the self experiences irreconcilable cognitive dissonance, (3) by simply living life itself, and (4) through conscious practice (therapeutic as much as spiritual).[101]

Hochachka says "most developmental psychologists seem to concur that a person cannot 'grow' another person." But things can be done to promote transformation. People can be "sensitized to their current and potential role in effecting positive change in their community, society, and environment."[102]

She continues: "Wilber describes other practices that help to foster shifts in self-stages and worldviews as 'Integral Life Practice'."[103] Earlier in this book an Integral Life Practice was talked about, and how it involved working on your body, mind, shadow, and spirit to promote growth.

Another way to promote transformation is to simply work on becoming healthier at the consciousness level where one is situated. This is called translation. Hochachka says those doing development can honor how people are seeing the world now, promote balancing of the quadrants, and encourage perspective-taking. She also writes, "Beck explains that the question is not 'how do you motivate people,' but 'how do you relate what you are doing to their natural motivational flows?'"[104]

Specifics of the Study in El Salvador

Hochachka spent nine months in Jiquilisco Bay, El Salvador, during 2000–2002. She started by doing house-to-house interviews to learn community values and establish relationships in the community. The next phase was to conduct two focus groups "using dialogue, group visioning, appreciative inquiry, and community mapping, to discuss common needs and visions, as well as to collaborate in responding to the community's pertinent concerns."[105] There was a third phase "including training workshops, meetings, fund-raising, cross-community exchanges, and soliciting assistance for specific initiatives."[106] She wrote, "the Integral framework helped us pay attention to exterior and interior dimensions of the research."[107] See Table 4.[108]

She stated:

> Community concerns (expressed in phases 1 and 2) included deforestation of the surrounding mangrove forest for fuel wood and construction materials, depletion of fish stocks, and limited economic alternatives for community members, particularly women. This was compounded by inadequate organization or capacity to address these problems.[109]

She decided to work with two focus groups. They were called the Fisherfolk and the Women's Council.

Fisherfolk Focus Group

This focus group consisted of six members of the fishery council, *Brisas del Mar*. This group was worried about low production in the lagoon:

> Thus, actions proposed by the group included (1) collaboration in fixing the border of the lagoon, (2) limiting the use of the smallest net size, and/or implementing fishing restrictions, and (3) boosting participation and motivation in problem-solving by strengthening internal organization.[110]

They proceeded to address these concerns.

Phase 1 Interviews and Meetings		Phase 2 Focus Groups		Phase 3 Exchanges and Actions	
Exterior	Interior	Exterior	Interior	Exterior	Interior
Open-ended questionnaire and meetings with leaders and local councils to understand the socioeconomic, ecological, political, and historical context of the community.	Using a conversation-style interview process, enabling interviewees to share personal stories, beliefs, and feelings. Learning about the "interior" context of the community (local beliefs, worldviews, and values). Building trust between our research team and the community. Sharing conversations on spirituality and (with some community members) prayers.	Dialoguing on issues and concerns, and collective problem-solving. Building capacity for group dialogue and collaboration. Using focus groups as a venue for social and technical capacity building (workshops on organization, fund-raising, and cooperative training).	Creating a "safe" and trusting space for exploring "self-in-relation." Bringing new ideas into dialogue, fostering an atmosphere of exploration, activating the "what if" mind. Building moral and emotional capacity (self-esteem and confidence to engage in the focus groups, and facilitating connection with others).	*Exchanges:* Sharing experiences and resources, learning other groups' challenges and successes. *Action:* Enabling research to be useful to meeting community's material needs.	*Exchanges:* Connecting different groups; fostering appreciation of "other" ways of being and perspectives; and providing opportunities to truly "see" these other perspectives. *Action:* Making action only one component of the project to point out the interior components.

Table 4: Exterior and Interior Dimensions of Methodologies Used in Each Phase of the Research.[111]

Women's Focus Group

A Women's Council Focus Group was formed. Their concern was a lack of stable work for women in the area. They decided that "since fish and shrimp would enter the lagoon naturally with the tides, the women could operate a small restaurant for fresh seafood dishes, and with reforesting of the area surrounding the lagoon, they could offer bird-watching canoe trips into the mangroves."[112] Also, "Their actions included forming a cooperative of 20 women, soliciting land for the initiative, improving group collaboration and organization, seeking financial support, and contracting technical studies for the construction, environmental impact, assessment, and management of the lagoon."[113]

Evaluation

Hochachka did "quantitative and participatory evaluations (personal interviews and group discussions) to gauge the exterior and interior outcomes of the research"[114] one year after the project. The following are her findings:

The fisherfolk group:

> (1) mitigated disputes between fishers by organizing more equitably, (2) effectively discussed and began implementing (short- and long-term) sustainable management strategies for the lagoon, (3) sought financial and technical support to identify and address the reasons for low production, and (4) boosted collaboration amongst fisherfolk.[115]

The women's group:

> (1) had begun the formation of a cooperative, (2) were attending capacity-building workshops, and (3) were working on raising funds and capacity to develop their lagoon and eco-tourism project. They had gone from being excluded in decision-making (and thus

also issues regarding family security) to having an unprecedented formal place in municipal governance and a nationally recognized legal presence as a cooperative.[116]

She writes:

The "interior" outcomes of the research were evident throughout the project as well. People had come together to discuss their differences and seek solidarity in their similarities, to address seriously their need for collaboration and organization, and to recognize each other's needs and value systems even if different from their own. The fisherfolk focus group recognized that family health was the common value that transcended their differences.[117]

Further results were that

in five months, the women had gone from discussing economic initiatives for two to three families to a larger, more inclusive project of 25 women that recognized the needs of the poorer families in the community.

The interior dimension of our work also related to the kinds of "capacity" that was developed through our process of working together.[118]

She further explains how this was done, and its effectiveness as a development strategy:

In our project, building technical and social capacity was facilitated through workshops, training, and (informal) mentoring; moral capacity was fostered through collective visioning and dialogue; and emotional capacity occurred through self-reflection and sharing. This "multifaceted" capacity-building was important in enabling the community to move beyond the dependency model of development to a more self-empowered and sustainable process.[119]

And regarding the possibility of transformation Hochachka says:

> Possibly the most profound interior outcome of the research was the subtle but meaningful shifts in worldviews. Throughout the project, we observed shifts in self-identity, morals, and perspectives, toward a more inclusive worldview that demonstrated more consideration for the less fortunate members of the community, for women in decision-making, for the surrounding ecosystems, and for neighboring communities.[120]

She then talks about the group moving to a more-complex stage of development that was worldcentric.[121]

She further talks about translation relating to transformation:

> To truly engage with inhabitants in community-directed work, the development practitioner must be able to "meet people where they are," in terms of both their value systems and their ways of "making meaning" building a bridge between existing worldviews and the emerging ones (as described by Kegan, 1994).[122]

She writes about her own growth as important to the project:

> My own self-development practices (yoga and meditation) during the project helped to foster the expansion of my own awareness, to be clear on my intention, to be receptive to intuition regarding the project, to surface my assumptions and locate my biases, and to be open to differences in perspective that I encountered.[123]

Hochachka returned to San Juan del Gozo Community, El Salvador, in February–March 2004, and in November 2005. She writes about the dominance of the lower-right quadrant in economic development viewed in 2004:

> recent political and economic trends have undermined some of the successes associated with the other quadrants. The Jiquilisco Bay region had begun to be developed as "the next Acapulco" for conventional tourism, which was then (and still is) a grave concern for local people whose main income comes from their natural habitat. This has caused the fishing cooperative to be wary of who they work with, causing what appeared to be a shift back toward sociocentric awareness, rather than a move toward worldcentric. The women's group has had an ongoing struggle with governmental institutions to legalize their cooperative, and the frustratingly slow and bureaucratic process has provoked frustration, lack of confidence as well as distrust with NGO CESTA.[124]

But in 2005 she observed that:

> the women's cooperative discontinued their work with CESTA, demonstrating an empowered stance that I commend them for, and yet continued collaboration with another NGO, the Salvadoran Women's Movement. The cooperative is now fully legalized and has secured access to land near their farms and adjacent to the mangrove, and is moving ahead with one of its original plans to raise livestock for dairy products, engage in the national economy, and support their families and the community as a whole.[125]

She sees this as "an expression of healthy sociocentrism, if not the emergence of early worldcentrism."[126] She writes "it is certainly an empowered and immense step for a group of women who formerly had no access to jobs, income, and thus no ability to affect family security."[127]

She suggested the regression, in 2004, as possibly being remedied by "sharing the approach I was using with other practitioners who could continue follow-up support with the community."[128] She writes:

> Development, therefore, means much more than accumulated wealth, built infrastructure, or economic growth, although it can include these, in one form or another. It is about aligning and attuning evolutionary unfolding of self, community, and environment, and recognizing where people are at and where their deepest division can carry them, creating spaces to explore self-in-relation, and consciously enabling self-growth and new discourse to flow through the collective into more compassionate action.[129]

Her study concludes thus:

> In San Juan del Gozo, our outcomes suggest that integrating interiority with the more exterior community development practices, individuals became more empowered in ways that contribute to community action and to averting ecological and social crisis, and the community became more able to address and move beyond these crises. Our experiences and outcomes in this case study suggest that sustainable community development is neither a far-off pipe dream nor a theoretical study, but an unfolding reality that is most successful when the interior and exterior aspects of individuals and communities are included and honored.[130]

This shows a more comprehensive approach to economic development and environmental economics that can be accomplished by emphasizing a couple of principles contained in this book. One is the inclusion of interior dimensions, and the other is an evolutionary progression relating to values and other developmental lines in the community being developed.

One final thought on environmental economics. Since many environmentalists think that governments do not seem to be effectively addressing climate change in a timely manner, nonprofit, or 10% maximum profit, economic entities may be a way to do so. For example, they might be able to provide wind and solar power for electricity for a cheaper price than using fossil fuels. This could make it more cost-effective for public utilities to move away from natural gas and coal-powered electrical plants. Nonprofit or 10% maximum profit economic organizations could be used to help solve other environmental problems. Hopefully, this will accelerate the move to a sustainable world.

7

Conclusion

LET US SUMMARIZE what our examination of evolutionary economics has proposed. We will talk about abundance, the specifics of how a Threefold State might look, and lastly how it could evolve, rather than being either imposed through revolution or mandated by the government. Still, laws will need to be passed in some cases.

A. Abundance

The first step is to start thinking about abundance. The current definition of economics talks about unlimited wants in the face of scarcity. We looked at unlimited wants as not being the case when it comes to goods and services. At some point, too much gets in the way or is unneeded. The evolutionary impulse to progress is always there, but this does not necessarily mean more material items. And as technology expands at an ever-increasing rate, production efficiency does also, and the population eventually peaks as countries develop and have lower birth rates. As a result, there should be plenty for all to live well.

B. The Threefold State and Purposive Economics

Steiner proposes dividing society into three parts: the economic, rights, and individual/cultural sectors. They would operate autonomously and negotiate with each other and other countries as if they were separate states. The following is a brief outline of the Threefold State as proposed in this book, plus summaries of the different sectors:

Threefold State Sectors

    Economic
        Purposive Economic Entities
                Working at a job that is your purpose
                Emphasis on the product or service
                Covering costs
                Do no harm to the environment
                Living wage
        Co-op banking for economic entities
        Change management in extreme cases

    Rights (to Ensure)
        Civil rights
        Healthcare
        Education
        Healthy environment
        Infrastructure
        Retirement and disability
        National defense, police, and fire protection
        Food
        Shelter

    Individual/Cultural (Institutions)
        Courts
        Education cooperatives

Healthcare cooperatives
Spiritual organizations
Co-op banking for individuals/families

1. Economic Sector

The economic part would be concerned with the production, circulation, and consumption of commodities. It is proposed that economic entities would move toward being purposive entities voluntarily. The major principles guiding these organizations would be having employees who are working at a job that is their passion, emphasizing making the best product or service possible, minimizing cost as opposed to maximizing profits, accounting for all costs to the best of an organization's ability including environmental ones, and paying employees a living wage.

Workers would be working at jobs that are their purpose. So, eliminating mindless assembly-line jobs through automation and even outsourcing and free trade would be seen as a positive thing in developed countries so workers can work at jobs that are their mission in life. It could be argued that everyone will want to be a rockstar, sports star, or movie star. But they should actually love music, playing a particular sport, or acting, and not be doing it for the glamor or high pay involved. Going along with doing a job that is a person's purpose, the employees of an organization would actually be excited about the good or service provided by the organization they work for. And the organization would be producing products/services that are good for their customers. For example, predatory lending, would not happen at a lending institution.

The economic entity should strive to also pay a living wage that allows its employees to live quite comfortably. And by minimizing costs as opposed to maximizing profits, lower prices and/or product improvement would become the norm for organizations. And with the reduced speculation in the stock market, and credit institutions becoming member-owned cooperatives, the business cycle should be moderated significantly.

2. Rights Sector

The primary focus of this sector would be rights such as guarantees of non-discrimination by age, race, sex, disability, or weight now. It would include items as are enumerated in the U.S. Bill of Rights currently regarding such things as a free press and free speech. But the rights sector would also provide for universal education and healthcare by providing funding mechanisms to acquire and distribute funds so that all may have access to these services. It would also provide mechanisms for income maintenance, such as unemployment and retirement/disability programs. Unemployment would hopefully be restricted mainly to former employees of economic organizations producing products no longer needed by the economy, so there would be an emphasis on retraining if needed. While economic entities would try to be conscious of their environmental footprint, ultimately the rights sector would be better able to assess what levels of pollution could be tolerated by the community as a whole, and this sector still would regulate to insure what safe levels of toxins would be. This sector would still be involved in providing infrastructure such as roads, canals, and water/sewer systems, among others. And the public safety right would be ensured by the national defense, police, and fire protection. Hopefully, government-provided food and shelter would be less needed as living wages, disability/retirement programs, unemployment benefits, retraining, and a reduced/eliminated business cycle come to fruition. Still, these may be needed as the economy evolves to a purposive one.

3. Individual/Cultural Sector

The individual/cultural sector would provide education, healthcare, and individual/family banking through consumer cooperatives. The individuals/families receiving these services could actively be involved for possibly a few hours a week in helping provide education/health services. In this way, they would have more knowledge of how these organizations operate, as well as be of service. But professionals would still be hired at a living wage to operate these organizations and be active on their boards of directors.

Courts would be also moved to the individual/cultural sector. Rudolf Steiner suggests that the directing body make judge appointments of five to ten years and that they be taken from a wide variety of professions.

C. Evolution, Not Revolution

The purposive economy should evolve, not be instituted by a revolution. Radical changes in laws should be avoided as much as possible. The individual/cultural sector, or interior quadrants, needs to be at a place where it is ready for change. That is why revolutions often fail: the "I" and "we" space is not ready for change. So, similar to how capitalism evolved, a purposive world should do so gradually. Advocating for more charter schools could help us evolve from public to private schools although possibly not allowing for-profit schools might help to make charter schools more purposive.

Some laws may need to be passed, though. Passing laws to outlaw economic entities, including unions, from contributing to political campaigns would help to separate the economics and rights sectors. This is advocated by many now, hence this may be a radical proposal that the individual/cultural sector is already on board with. Current healthcare in the United States is controversial now, hence reforming the Affordable Care Act may well be very possible. Moving the court system to the private/cultural sector would need to be considered very carefully since it would be the most radical of changes to the social order proposed here.

This is a vision of how a new economic system could evolve as the information age progresses.

D. Conscious Capitalism

There is a movement within the integral community called Conscious Capitalism. There is a book titled *Conscious Capitalism* by Whole Foods founder John Mackey and marketing professor Rajendra S. Sisodia, and an organization by that name promotes the principles of the movement. The four principles from the organization's website are:

Higher Purpose — "Businesses should exist for reasons beyond just making a profit. 'We need red blood cells to live (the same way a business needs profits to live), but the purpose of life is more than to make red blood cells (the same way, the purpose of business is more than simply to generate profits).' — R. Edward Freedman, University of Virginia Darden School of Business professor. Knowing WHY your business exists provides you with a compass to find and stay focused on achieving your True North (Higher Purpose). Profit is a means to the end of purpose for conscious businesses."[131]

Conscious Leadership — "Conscious businesses cannot exist without Conscious Leaders. Conscious Leaders focus on 'we,' rather than 'me.' They inspire positive transformation and bring out the best in those around them. They keep the business focused on its Higher Purpose, and support the people within the organization to create value for all of the organization's stakeholders. They recognize the integral role of culture and purposefully cultivate a Conscious Culture of trust and care."[132]

Stakeholder Orientation — "When you tug at a single thing in nature, you find it attached to the rest of the world. — John Muir, Pioneering naturalist. Such is the case with business, which operates from an ecosystem of your employees, customers, suppliers, investors, society, and environment . . . sometimes this even includes your competition. Conscious businesses value and care for EVERYONE in their ecosystem, motivating their stakeholders by creating 'win–win–win' outcomes for all who are impacted by their business."[133]

Conscious Culture — "Culture is the embodied values, principles and practices underlying the social fabric of a business, signaling 'how' business is done. The culture of your business is its heartbeat.

Without a healthy one, the business will ultimately fail. A Conscious Culture fosters love and care and builds trust between a company's team members and its other stakeholders. Conscious Culture also includes accountability, transparency, integrity, loyalty, egalitarianism, fairness, and personal growth, acting as an energizing and unifying force that truly brings a conscious business to life."[134]

The first higher purpose principle comes close to talking about purposive economic organizations in a way, by emphasizing that the profit motive should not be primary. But the problems that occur when the organization, or the investors, forgets this and lets greed take over would still be there. The instability of the current capitalist system would be more likely to persist. Stockholders looking for an unearned increment and the very competitive world of stockbrokers both make the devolution into greed, resulting in stock market bubbles and recessions, more possible. This has been shown already to be a problem: investors forced Whole Foods to sell out to Amazon due to the profit motive. The other three principles of conscious leadership, stakeholder orientation, and consciousness culture could easily be part of purposive organizations.

E. Not Socialism or Too Idealistic

When the idea of moving toward a 10% maximum profit world is mentioned, some might automatically call it socialism. But it is not since there would be less government, and the economy would be more separate from the rights sector than is currently the case. Some of the values espoused in this book are similar to those of socialism, though. There would be more equality and more stability, and a world governed under these ideas would be better for the environment. These are problems that socialism tries to solve, but purposive organizations would let the genius of the private sector do it for the most part. A purposive economy is a harmonious solution to the problems of capitalism and socialism.

Are the ideas too idealistic? An emphasis has been put on evolution, but mankind's consciousness is progressing at an ever-faster rate, as evidenced by the Years Ago Started column in Table 1, so the time may well be right for us to be more in tune with our ideals. And without mandating purposive entities, as communism did with socialism, the worst that could happen is that some organizations could try it, and if it did not work, only those organizations that did not succeed would experience the consequences of the failure. The problems of a totalitarian regime would not be experienced by a whole country. But if the ideas proposed in this book work well, a more ideal world could come about sooner than one might imagine.

Endnotes

1. Robert L. Heilbroner, *The Worldly Philosophers* (New York: A Clarion Book Published by Simon and Schuster, 1967), 13–14.
2. Ken Wilber, "Introduction to Integral Theory and Practice: IOS Basic and the AQAL Map," *AQAL: Journal of Integral and Practice* 1, no. 1 (Spring 2005): 24.
3. Wilber, "Introduction to Integral Theory and Practice," 25.
4. Roger L. Miller, *Economics Today, 18*th ed. (Boston: Pearson Education, Inc. 2016), 2.
5. Wilber, "Introduction to Integral Theory and Practice," 23.
6. Wilber, "Introduction to Integral Theory and Practice," 24.
7. Wilber, "Introduction to Integral Theory and Practice," 25.
8. Miller, *Economics Today,* 12.
9. Jessica Roemischer, "The Never-Ending Upward Quest: A WIE Editor Encounters the Practical and Spiritual Wisdom of Spiral Dynamics—An Interview with Dr. Don Beck," *What Is Enlightenment?,* no. 22 (Fall/Winter 2002): 108, 109.
10. Ken Wilber, *Integral Psychology* (Boston: Shambhala Publications, 2000), 214.
11. Wilber, *Integral Psychology*, 201. Note that the different levels of the concrete operational and formal operational stages are not detailed here, and that Wilber's term vision logic is used in place of polyvalent logic. Other stages are not included and are not necessary for the purposes of this book.

12. Wilber, *Integral Psychology*, 212

13. Wilber, *Integral Psychology*, 48–52.

14. Ken Wilber, "The Economics of Being Integral," accessed June 2019, https://integrallife.com/the-economics-of-being-integral-2/.

15. Wilber, *Integral Psychology*, 52.

16. Wilber, *Integral Psychology*, 50.

17. "Agriculture in the United States: Employment," Wikipedia, 2019, accessed November 2019, http://en.wikipedia.org/wiki/Agriculture_in_ the_United_States.

18. *Merriam-Webster*, s.v. "greed," accessed June 2019, https://www.merriam-webster.com/dictionary.

19. Adam Smith, *The Wealth of Nations* (London: J. M. Dent & Sons, 1910), 13.

20. Miller, *Economics Today*, 603.

21. Ken Wilber, *Integral Spirituality* (Boston: Shambhala Publications, 2006), 85.

22. Ken Wilber, *Sex, Ecology, Spirituality* (Boston: Shambhala Publications, 1995), 165.

23. Wilber, *Sex, Ecology, Spirituality*, 179.

24. Wilber, *Sex, Ecology, Spirituality*, 173.

25. Wilber, *Sex, Ecology, Spirituality*, 189.

26. Wilber, *Sex, Ecology, Spirituality*, 173.

27. Miller, *Economics Today*, 6.

28. Miller, *Economics Today*, 10.

29. Wilber, *Sex, Ecology, Spirituality*, 173.

30. Wilber, *Sex, Ecology, Spirituality*, 205–208.

31. "Economics: Key Takeaways," Investopedia, 2019, accessed June 2019, http://www.investopedia.com/terms/e/economics.asp.

32. Miller, *Economics Today*, 29.

33. Louise Hay, *You Can Heal Your Life* (New York: Hay House, Inc., 2004), 118.

34. "World Population Prospects 2017," United Nations, 2017, accessed September 2018, https://population.un.org/wpp/.

35. United Nations, "World Population Prospects 2017."

36. Michael E. Zimmerman, "The Singularity: A Crucial Phase in Divine Self-Actualization," *Cosmos and History: The Journal of Natural and Social Philosophy*, 4, nos. 1–2 (2008): 347.

37. Rudolf Steiner, *The Threefold State—The True Aspect of the Social Question* (London: George Allen and Unwin, Ltd., 1920), 55.

38. CGP Grey, "Humans Need Not Apply," 2014, accessed July 2019, https://www.bing.com/videos/search?q=%22Humans+Need+Not+Apply%22+&view=detail&mid=4027A7C065FFC5103AE84027A7C065FFC5103AE8&FORM=VIRE.

39. Wilber, *Integral Psychology*, 212.

40. Miller, *Economics Today,* 30.

41. Yannick Griep et al., "The Effects of Unemployment and Perceived Job Insecurity: A Comparison of Their Association with Psychological and Somatic Complaints, Self-Rated Health and Life Satisfaction," *International Archives of Occupational and Environmental Health* 89, no. 1 (January 2016): 147, accessed July 2019, https://doi.org/10.1007/s00420-015-1059-5.

42. Alice Tuovila, "Normal Profit," 2020, accessed December 2021, https://www.investopedia.com/terms/n/normal_profit.asp.

43. Miller, *Economics Today*, 487.

44. Miller, *Economics Today*, 487.

45. Andrew Sather, "What is a Good Net Profit Margin? 20 Years of Data from the S & P 500," 2020, accessed December 2021, https://einvesting-forbeginners.com/good-net-profit-margin-dataset/.

46. Amy K. Glasmeier, "Living Wage Calculator," 2018, accessed July 2019, http://livingwage.mit.edu/.

47. Jamie Raskin, "The Rise of Benefit Corporations," *The Nation* (June 27, 2011), accessed July 2019, https://www.thenation.com/article/rise-benefit-corporations/.

48. "State-by-State Status of Legislation," Benefit Corporation, 2019, accessed July 2019, https://benefitcorp.net/policymakers/state-by-state-status.

48. Samer Abu-Saifan, "Social Entrepreneurship: Definition and Boundaries," accessed July 2019, http://timereview.ca/article/523.

49. Steiner, *The Threefold State*, 95.

50. Steiner, *The Threefold State*, 96.
51. Steiner, *The Threefold State*, 96, 97.
52. Steiner, *The Threefold State*, 57.
53. Steiner, *The Threefold State*, 67.
54. Steiner, *The Threefold State*, 68.
55. Steiner, *The Threefold State*, 87.
56. Steiner, *The Threefold State*, 88.
57. Steiner, *The Threefold State*, 171, 172.
58. Steiner, *The Threefold State*, 73.
59. Steiner, *The Threefold State*, 133.
60. Steiner, *The Threefold State*, 77.
61. Steiner, *The Threefold State*, 157, 158.
62. Steiner, *The Threefold State*, 177, 178.
63. Ken Wilber, Terry Patten, Adam Leonard, and Marco Morelli, *Integral Life Practice* (Boston: Integral Books, 2008), 15, 16.
64. Miller, *Economics Today*, 454.
65. Miller, *Economics Today*, 699.
66. Wilber, *Sex, Ecology, Spirituality*, 159–164, 178–184.
67. Wilber, *Sex, Ecology, Spirituality*, 387–389.
68. "Facts Over Time—Women in the Labor Force (Labor Force Participation Rate by Sex, Race and Hispanic Ethnicity)," United States Department of Labor—Women's Bureau, accessed July 2019, https://www.dol.gov/wb/stats/NEWSTATS/facts/women_lf.htm#two.
69. Bridget T. Long, "The College Completion Landscape: Trends, Challenges, and Why it Matters," May 25, 2018, accessed July 2019, https://www.thirdway.org/report/the-college-completion-landscape-trends-challenges-and-why-it-matters.
70. Steiner, *The Threefold State*, 62.
71. Steiner, *The Threefold State*, 80, 81.
72. Steiner, *The Threefold State*, 112.
73. Miller, *Economics Today*, 673.
74. The development of where an economic entity will produce takes a few chapters in economics textbooks, so explaining this fully would take much more space, and would add little to the mission of this book.

75. Miller, *Economics Today*, 1.
76. Miller, *Economics Today*, 336.
77. Miller, *Economics Today*, 337.
78. Miller, *Economics Today*, 337.
79. Miller, *Economics Today*, 338.
80. John Stuart Mill, *Principles of Political Economy* (New York: D. Appleton & Company, 1885), 161.
81. Henry George, *The Complete Works of Henry George: The Land Question* (New York: Doubleday, Page & Company, 1904), 43.
82. Jürgen Habermas, *Communication and the Evolution of Society* (Boston: Beacon Press, 1979), 134.
83. Mitch Galloway, "Michigan's Gain? State More Resilient to NAFTA Withdrawal Than Expected, Per U-M Projections," 2018, accessed July 2019, https://mibiz.com/item/25688-michigan-s-gain-state-more-resilient-to-nafta-withdrawal-than-expected,-per-u-m-projections.
84. Shawn Esborjorn-Hargens and Michael Zimmerman, eds., *Integral Ecology* (Boston and London: Integral Books, 2011), 489–530.
85. Gail Hochachka, "Integrating Interiority in Sustainable Community Development: A Case Study with San Juan del Gozo Community, El, Salvador," in *Integral Ecology*, eds. Shawn Esborjorn-Hargens and Michael Zimmerman (Boston and London: Integral Books, 2011), 393, 394.
86. Hochachka, "Integrating Interiority ," 394.
87. Hochachka, "Integrating Interiority," 396.
88. Hochachka, "Integrating Interiority," 396.
89. Hochachka, "Integrating Interiority," 398.
90. Hochachka, "Integrating Interiority," 398. Note that an orange altitude relates to orange values.
91. Hochachka, "Integrating Interiority," 398.
92. Hochachka, "Integrating Interiority," 399, 400.
93. Hochachka, "Integrating Interiority," 401.
94. This relates to blue or less-complex values.
95. Hochachka, "Integrating Interiority," 403, 404.
96. Hochachka, "Integrating Interiority," 403.
97. Hochachka, "Integrating Interiority," 404.

98. Hochachka, "Integrating Interiority," 404.
99. Hochachka, "Integrating Interiority," 406.
100. Hochachka, "Integrating Interiority," 407.
101. Hochachka, "Integrating Interiority," 407.
102. Hochachka, "Integrating Interiority," 408.
103. Hochachka, "Integrating Interiority," 408.
104. Hochachka, "Integrating Interiority," 410.
105. Hochachka, "Integrating Interiority," 411.
106. Hochachka, "Integrating Interiority," 411.
107. Hochachka, "Integrating Interiority," 411.
108. Hochachka, "Integrating Interiority," 412.
109. Hochachka, "Integrating Interiority," 413.
110. Hochachka, "Integrating Interiority," 413, 414.
111. Hochachka, "Integrating Interiority," 412.
112. Hochachka, "Integrating Interiority," 414.
113. Hochachka, "Integrating Interiority," 414, 415
114. Hochachka, "Integrating Interiority," 415.
115. Hochachka, "Integrating Interiority," 415.
116. Hochachka, "Integrating Interiority," 415.
117. Hochachka, "Integrating Interiority," 415, 416.
118. Hochachka, "Integrating Interiority," 416.
119. Hochachka, "Integrating Interiority," 416.
120. Hochachka, "Integrating Interiority," 417.
121. Hochachka, "Integrating Interiority," 417.
122. Hochachka, "Integrating Interiority," 417.
123. Hochachka, "Integrating Interiority," 420.
124. Hochachka, "Integrating Interiority ," 422.
125. Hochachka, "Integrating Interiority," 422.
126. Hochachka, "Integrating Interiority," 422.
127. Hochachka, "Integrating Interiority," 422.
128. Hochachka, "Integrating Interiority," 423.
129. Hochachka, "Integrating Interiority," 421.

130. Hochachka, "Integrating Interiority," 424.

131. "What is Conscious Capitalism?" Conscious Capitalism, accessed November, 2019, http://www.consciouscapitalism.org/.

132. Conscious Capitalism, "What is Conscious Capitalism?"

133. Conscious Capitalism, "What is Conscious Capitalism?"

134. Conscious Capitalism, "What is Conscious Capitalism?"

About the Author

JENDEN HUNT WAS an economist for the State of Michigan for 23 years and has taught economics at Schoolcraft College since 2003. She has extensively read the work of the integral philosopher Ken Wilber and Anthroposophy founder Rudolf Steiner. She has attended numerous conferences at the Integral Institute and has been the organizer of The Ann Arbor Ken Wilber Meetup Group since 2005. She may be contacted at the website GraelPublishing.com. and e-mailed at huntjenden@gmail.com.

www.ingramcontent.com/pod-product-compliance
Lightning Source LLC
Chambersburg PA
CBHW071430210326

41597CB00020B/3735